At the Inland Sea

A student prepares to go
It is exam day
A stranger enters
There is danger outside
The stranger makes a request that seems both odd and useless . . .

Edward Bond was born and educated in London. His plays
include *The Pope's Wedding* (Royal Court Theatre, 1962), *Saved*
(Royal Court, 1965), *Early Morning* (Royal Court, 1968), *Narrow
Road to the Deep North* (Belgrade Theatre, Coventry, 1968; Royal
Court, 1969), *Black Mass* (Sharpeville Commemoration Evening,
Lyceum Theatre, 1970), *Passion* (CND Rally, Alexandra Palace,
1971), *Lear* (Royal Court, 1971), *The Sea* (Royal Court, 1973),
Bingo (Northcott, Exeter, 1973; Royal Court, 1974), *The Fool*
(Royal Court, 1975), *The Bundle* (RSC Warehouse, 1978), *The
Woman* (National Theatre, 1978), *The Worlds* (New Half Moon
Theatre, London, 1981), *Restoration* (Royal Court, 1981), *Summer*
(National Theatre, 1982), *Derek* (RSC Youth Festival, The
Other Place, Stratford-upon-Avon, 1982), *The Cat* (produced in
Germany as *The English Cat* by the Stuttgart Opera, 1983), *Human
Cannon* (Quantum Theatre, Manchester, 1986), *The War Plays*
(*Red Black and Ignorant, The Tin Can People* and *Great Peace*), which
were staged as a trilogy by the RSC at the Barbican Pit in 1985,
Jackets (Leicester, Haymarket, 1989), *September* (Canterbury
Cathedral, 1989), *In the Company of Men* (Paris, 1992; RSC at the
Barbican Pit, 1996), *At the Inland Sea* (toured by Big Brum
Theatre-in-Education, 1995); *Olly's Prison* (BBC 2 Television,
1993), *Tuesday* (BBC Schools TV, 1993). His *Theatre Poems and
Songs* were published in 1978, *Poems 1978–1985* in 1987, and his
recent play *Coffee* in 1995.

Tony Coult is a writer and teacher. He has worked as a
performer with young people's theatre companies, such as Leeds
TiE, Perspectives and Interplay, and is a Visiting Director at
Rose Bruford College. His radio work includes drama for BBC
Radios 4 and 5, and dramatizations of young people's fiction. His
published work includes *The Plays of Edward Bond* (Methuen) and
Engineers of the Imagination (Methuen) as well as original drama for
schools and colleges.

Edward Bond

AT THE INLAND SEA

a play for young people

Notes and Commentary
by **Tony Coult**

Methuen Drama

A Methuen Modern Play

First published in Great Britain 1997
by Methuen
Random House, 20 Vauxhall Bridge Road, London
SW1V 2SA
Random House Australia (Pty) Limited,
20 Alfred Street, Milsons Point, Sydney, New South Wales
2061, Australia
Random House New Zealand Limited, 18 Poland Road,
Glenfield, Auckland 10, New Zealand
Random House South Africa (Pty) Limited, Endulini,
5A Jubilee Road, Parktown 2193, South Africa

ISBN 0 413 70630 3

A CIP catalogue record for this book
is available at the British Library

Typeset by Wilmaset Ltd, Birkenhead, Wirral
Printed and bound in Great Britain by Cox & Wyman Ltd,
Reading, Berkshire

Contents

For Thomas

At the Inland Sea

At the Inland Sea was first presented by Big Brum on 16 October 1995 at Broadway School, Aston, Birmingham, prior to a tour of the Midlands. The company comprised Bobby Colvill, Mandy Finney and Terina Talbot (actor–teachers); Geoff Gillham, director; Michael Irvine, designer–stage manager.

Characters

Boy
Mother
Woman
Man on Roof
Old Woman
Soldiers, People

Note

In the original production the Man on Roof, soldiers and people were performed by taped voices.

One

*The **Boy**'s bedroom. A chair. On it a school jacket, school case and school books. Beside it the **Boy**'s shoes.*

*The **Boy** enters. He carries a mug of tea. He puts the mug on the floor. He sits on the bed and puts on his shoes.*

*The **Mother** is heard calling from another room.*

Mother   I never did exams. Schools didn't have them then. Not proper exams. Did some papers at the end of term. They didn't give you passes and certificates. Just a report.

*The **Boy** finishes putting on his shoes. For a moment he stares in front of him. Then he picks up a book, finds his place and reads.*

*The **Mother** comes in.*

Mother   O he's studying now it's too late. Should've done that when I told you. Don't forget to make your bed. Don't leave it for me to come home to. (*The **Boy** goes on reading. She stares at him for a moment.*) You're not worried?

Boy   I'm trying to read this.

Mother   You don't have to worry. The teacher said you'll pass. As long as you concentrate. That's your trouble. Always staring out the window. I think you'll end up a window cleaner. No good just scraping through. You need good passes. Keep up with the high-flyers. (*The **Boy** reads.*) Time you were in your jacket. Get there early. Give yourself time to settle down and get your ideas sorted out. I gave that jacket a good brush last night. You feel better when you make a good impression. I wish I was doing exams. Working for my boss – you need a degree in slavery. God knows I've done the studying.

*The **Mother** goes out. The **Boy** puts down the book, stands and picks up the mug. He drinks.*

Mother (*off*)   Mrs Lacey said her Ron's worried sick. He's another one who can't be told. Up all hours. Listening to his music. Now he's facing the consequences.

*The **Boy** starts to tremble slightly. He steadies the mug with both hands and wedges it against his chest. His head rises a little as if he looked at something beyond the room but his eyes focus on space just in front of him.*

Mother (*off*)   Always shouting. Barging up and down the street on his skates. I went in the supermarket. He came round the corner on his skates. Pushing a trolley! I couldn't believe my eyes. The old people were terrified. The assistant manager said if they saw him in there again he'd send for the police. He's lucky I'm not marking his papers. I wouldn't even give him nought.

*The **Boy** is frozen. Behind him a **Woman** has risen from the bed. She wears old ragged clothes and carries a baby wrapped in a bundle. She and the baby – their clothes, hair and skin – seem to be cut from the same dull cloth. The **Woman** walks across the room nursing the baby.*

Woman (*half singsong*)   The world's a stone. The world's a stone.

Mother (*off*)   Pity they don't give prizes for shouting. He'd come top.

Woman (*as if rehearsing a speech*)   Let me work for you. I'll do the housework. Or work out in the yard. I'll do anything that's to be done. You won't kill my baby. People would know – you'd be blamed even after you're dead – for ever. Let me work for you. My baby won't annoy you. It doesn't cry. Look it's asleep. It's a – (*Stops.*) No don't beg. Give them something. What? No money. No clothes. (*Rehearsing again.*) I can't work without my baby. It'd fret. If you want the work done I must have my baby with me. (*To baby.*) They won't kill you! There must be something to – (*Half singsong.*) The world's a stone. The world's a stone.

*The **Boy** has gone to the chair. He sits huddled, clasping the cup.*

*The **Mother** comes in.*

Mother I'll make your bed this once. Once, mind. Not making a habit of it. (*Starts to make the bed.*) You make it tomorrow.

Woman (*rehearsing her speech*) I'm fit and strong. I look weak because I – (*Half singsong.*) The world's a stone. The world's a stone. (*Looks into the distance.*) The lorries were parked all night on the square. We can't go back to the house. Soldiers on the doors. Neighbours leaning out of the windows. The end of the street's still empty. Perhaps they won't come today. They'll come tomorrow. If I have one more day I can think. There must be something I can do. They'll come, they'll come.

Mother (*passing the* **Boy**) Move. You're in the way.

Slowly the **Boy**'s *arm straightens – he holds out the cup to the* **Woman**.

Mother (*making the bed*) If the boss says anything to me today I'll tell him what's what. Look Mr Simpson it's not right picking on your best worker. You never heard the customers complain. Can I help it if they want to chat? They tell me about their grandkids and next-door. Some of them come in for things they don't really want – just to say hello. I give them a smile even when we're rushed. That's what I'll tell him. Only I won't. Say anything they hold it against you later. If I wasn't there he'd pick on someone else. Least it sends you to school in a clean shirt. Look at the state of this pillow-slip! You're not ending up in a dead-end job like I did.

The tea starts to drip from the cup and then slowly spill.

Woman If they saw your face they couldn't hurt you. If they saw your little hands. They don't look. If they heard you cry. You don't cry. I didn't teach you how. I can't cry any more. I cried all my tears. That's why I don't look at you now. I can't feed you. I can't wash and change you. Why should I look at you? I'll never look at you again. If I tried it would hurt. I'd drop you at my feet in the street. They'd sweep you up with the rubbish. They're going to kill you … (*Rehearsing.*) We had training in home-care at school. I could get references. (*Half singsong*.) The world's a stone. The world's a stone.

Mother (*finishes making the bed*)   There. Your turn tomorrow. (*Sees the* **Boy** *is holding out the cup*.) Want more tea? You know where the kettle is. You don't have to study geography to find the kitchen. (*Starts to go*.) I'm not your servant. If I start encouraging you in bad habits God knows where it'll end. (*Pillow-slip*.) I'll change this. It'll have to last you next week.

The **Mother** *goes out with the pillow-slip*.

Woman   I used to tell you stories. You were too little to understand. You knew my voice. You were so quiet. So still. I loved you even more then – I can never show my gratitude. (*Rehearsing*.) I'll carry heavy things. Fetch the shopping. You'll have my baby as hostage: I'll have to work. I'll live off scraps and snatch a half-hour's sleep in a corner with my baby . . . (*Half singsong*.) The world's a stone. The world's a stone. What can I do? I can't look at my baby. I can't look at the sky. I can't look at the end of the street. The lorries will come round the corner. If I told the soldiers a story. The right story. They'd listen like you did. They'd be still like you were. They couldn't kill you. All the soldiers sitting round me on the ground with their rifles. I'd hold you in my lap and tell the story. What story? . . . Tell me a story my precious. You know stories. That's why you were so still. Tell me a story – and you'll live. They'll hurt you, precious. You'll whine. (*Imitates a baby*.) 'It hurts, it hurts' . . . It can't speak. (*Picks up a stone and asks it:*) Tell me a story! Tell me a story! Their uniforms are your colour. Tell me the story. The world's a stone, the world's a stone! The things you've seen – you must know the story! It's crying! The stone! Crying! No! My tears! I cried! My tears fell on it . . . (*Drops stone*.) My baby's going to die. (*To the baby*.) I'll look at you when you're dead. They'll throw you on the heap of dead babies. I'll climb on the heap and look at all the faces. How will I know it's you? All their faces are the same when they're killed. I'll know your hands. The hands will be the same! How will I know?

(*Looks round, half calls.*) Tell me a story! I'll pay! (*Looks for something to pay with, feels inside the bundle.*) Look! – dirt from my baby's face! I'll pay you with that! Look how fine and soft and black! You could put it in a ring. When you went to heaven you could show it – they'd cry and let you in. (*Looks up.*) And all the sky – when it's black – is that dirt from the faces of dying babies? (*Picks dirt from the ground.*) Look! Dirt – to pay for the story! My baby was carried over that dirt! Take it! It's worth the story! Don't let them kill my baby!

Mother *comes in. She carries a clean pillow-slip.*

Mother I'm not making your tea. No time now anyway. If you don't get a move on you'll be late. Don't say I didn't warn you the – O God! What's that – ? You spilt the tea! Is that tea? Look at the mess! What d'you think you're – ! Well I'm not clearing it up! You clear up after yourself. If you – (*Controls herself.*) Look at the mess! Honestly at times you're worse than a baby. Give me that cup. Your nice trousers all splashed! I wanted you to look nice today. Give me the cup. I'll make you a fresh one. Not sending you out today without your tea. You'll come home this evening and realise how clever you are. You'll do fine! What is it? Aren't you well? You're shaking . . . O this is silly. I'm not giving in to it. It's always something with you! I worked hard for these exams. Gave you all the extras. Books. Bits and pieces for your computer. I had to do overtime. You're taking the exams for *me* – not just you. I'm going to pass. I deserve it. I'm up to here with your selfishness. If I did the exams I'd pass ignorant as I am. I can't afford not to. I know what it means to go without. You've been cosseted. I'm fed up with being on the bottom of the heap. I want a bit of life for a change. So no more of this bloody nonsense! And clear up this mess for a start! I want it done before you go through that door. Or you'll get the back of my hand and you can go to school with the marks of my fingers on your face. Let them all know!

Boy Tell me a story.

Mother You're trembling. (*Cup.*) Give me the – let go. Let it go!

The **Mother** *pulls at the cup. The* **Boy** *holds on to it. She lets it go.*

Mother   ... You're upsetting me luvvy. What is it? You won't pass. Is that it? You won't sit the exams because you know you'll ... (*Sits on the side of the bed.*) What've I done? I pushed you too hard. I should've given you your head like Mrs Lacey did her boy. He'll pass. She'll be up and down the street all smiles. The school said let you set your own pace. I don't know what that means. How could I tell if you were studying? I don't understand your books. If I'd left you to get on with it nothing'd've been done. Now this! (*Angry.*) Give me that cup! There's nothing wrong with you! Nervous, all right – but this is play-acting! Give me that cup! And clear up this mess! I'm not having it paddled all over my floor! I don't care how late you are!

The **Mother** *pulls at the cup. The* **Boy** *holds on to it. She drags him to his feet and along a few paces. His face is expressionless. She jerks at the cup – it falls to the floor and breaks.*

Mother   Now look what you done!

Half pause.

Boy   Tell me a story.

Mother   Don't stand there like that. Can't you hear me? I'm afraid to touch you. Luvvy, luvvy. You broke the cup ... All this fuss – their stupid exams. You can sit them later. They can arrange it if you're not well ... Is it going to be like this all your life? I pity your kids and the woman you'll marry. When a difficulty turns up you just pack it in? You carry on like this you'll end up on the street. Other kids don't do this to their mothers ... Sit there for a bit. It'll pass. You're better already. The cup wasn't expensive. (*She picks up the broken pieces of cup.*) ... I don't know how to get it right. When you were little, the slightest cough – I imagined the worst. You were going to die. Silly – there was never anything wrong with you ... I'll ring the school. You can't go in today. Lie down.

The **Mother** *covers the* **Boy** *with the bed-cover. She stares at him.*

Woman The lorries are turning into the street. The soldiers' faces crowded in the windscreens. They've seen us.

Mother If you felt a bit better in a few minutes – it's still not too late to go in. Then you'd know one way or the other. I can't go through this again. (*No response.*) I'll ring.

The **Mother** *goes out. Lorries. Military orders in a strange, unclear language. A man laughs. A few women call. Doors slam. Something is broken. A small incident involving a few people. The voices and sounds are heard as the* **Woman** *talks.*

Woman I knew they'd come, I knew they'd come. (*Calls.*) Work! Woman for work! Looking for work! I'm not to be taken. Don't come near! The baby's dead! Contagious disease! Don't touch it! It can't go in the lorry!

Soldiers are coming towards her.

Woman No! No! If you touch my baby I'll – (*Whispered violent aside to the baby.*) I can see their claws! They're beasts in clothes! (*Shouts.*) Work! Work! Work! (*Whispered violent aside to the baby.*) I can see their teeth! Flesh still on them! (*Shouts.*) I took it to the cemetery! I dropped it in your pits! It touched the dead! It's foul! – Touch it! Touch it! Touch it! Then fondle your babes! Kiss your wives! Eat with it on your hands! Work! Work! Work!

The **Woman** *struggles with the soldiers.*

Woman Listen! Once upon a time. Once there was a prince! Sit! Sit on the ground! An old woman – her children – they lived by the sea! (*Shout of terror.*) He's put a gun in its face! No no let me go! Your officers won't know! Then you won't be blamed for killing us – the blame will last for ever – let me go – and be blessed for –. The stones don't want my baby's blood on them! It'd stay there for ever! Pity the stones!

The **Woman** *fights the soldiers. They drag her away.*

Woman (*whispered fierce aside to the baby*) They're dragging us to their lair to eat! (*Shouts.*) Not men! Beasts!

The **Woman** *goes out. The* **Boy** *lies still on the bed. The* **Mother** *comes in with a floor cloth.*

Mother   The doctor's phoned. And the school. (*Mops up the tea.*) It'll leave a stain. If the doctor sees it he'll get all sorts of ideas. God knows where they'd put you. It's nerves. The secretary at the school said there's always one or two. She said they're the brightest. I'll phone the boss. Tell him I won't be in. Give him something real to moan about. It can't be anything serious if it comes on so sudden. If the doctor says you're well enough, I'll go in for the half-day. Don't want to lose a whole day's money.

*The **Mother** finishes mopping up the tea.*

Two

*The **Boy** lies in his bed staring at the ceiling. The **Mother** comes in. She straightens the bed.*

Mother   Nothing to worry about. The doctor's pleased with you. He says you're making progress. He changed your prescription. I'll take it to the chemist. How d'you feel? (*No response. She stares at him in silence for a moment.*) Can't you remember anything?

Boy   No.

Mother   Did you feel dizzy? (*No answer.*) Couldn't you hear me when I spoke?

Boy   I don't know.

Mother   You must remember the cup. You sat there with it in your hands. The tea was on the floor. First you wouldn't give me the cup. Then you threw it at me. (*No response.*) I've got to go in. It's two days. I daren't ask for more time. They don't carry extra staff to fill in. I'll get you something to eat before I go.

Boy (*flatly*)   No.

Mother   You must eat. That's not asking too much! (*Pause.*) I'll put it in the micro. You just have to go down and switch it on.

Boy   Tell me a story.

Mother   I'll try to get back a bit early. The doctor wants you to sleep. I wish you wouldn't keep saying that. I wanted to ask the doctor about it but I felt too embarrassed. (*Slight pause.*) I haven't got time to tell stories. What sort of story? (*She stares at him. He doesn't answer.*) You *are* an obstinate boy when you want to be. You get pleasure out of it. (*No answer.*) The doctor says no books. That includes stories. Shall I bring the telly up? . . . You want to be careful what you're getting yourself into. Something you may regret. (*Pause.*) You're past stories your age . . . You must've had a blackout.

Boy   Tell me a story.

Mother   What sort of story? (*Silence.*) If you don't know why d'you keep asking? You're no more ill than I am. The doctor says it's overwork and stress. If that's ill we're all ill. Asking for silly stories! At least if you ate I'd know you had food inside you. I suppose you want me to worry about that all day? If I don't keep my mind on the job I get the sack. I'll try to ring. If the phone rings you answer. You won't be asleep. I'll pop out and phone dinnertime when the boss is in the pub. I can't even ask the neighbours to look in. Just what they'd like! Come in, all sympathy, mop your brow – and eyes everywhere. Next thing we're burgled. I suppose I could take you down to the hospital. I don't know if the doctor's any good. They pass their exams but that means nothing nowadays. Hardly have time to get through the door. (*Silence.*) I've got to go. (*Silence.*) Sometimes I wonder what my life's for. What the point of it is. No one told me.

Silence.

Boy   Tell me a story.

Silence.

Mother (*slight sigh*)   I know what it is. You get something in your head. Like a tune in the back of your mind. When you try to sing it it's gone. The doctor says your temperature's still a bit high. Makes your mind race . . . I used to play in this backyard. With a school-friend. We said we'd keep in touch.

Made a vow and spat on a coin. Haven't seen her for years. Can't remember her name. I used to know it as well as I know my own. Her mother told us the story.

Boy   What was it about?

Mother   I expect it was something silly. If I remembered it I'll be disappointed.

Boy   What was it –

Mother   I don't know.

Boy   Tell me.

Mother   There was a room . . . and children . . . one had a blue jumper.

*The **Woman** enters carrying the baby.*

Mother   I remember . . .

Boy   What?

Mother   She knitted. While she told us about the jumper she knitted it.

Boy   Yes?

Mother   I don't remember any more. I forget.

Boy   But you said she –

Mother   I forget! It's silly, silly! She knitted the jumper for my friend. It was blue. That's the story. Now leave me alone.

*The **Boy** picks up his book and searches for his place.*

Mother   The doctor said no books.

*The **Boy** reads.*

Mother   Why must you punish me?

*The **Mother** turns her back on him, lost in angry thought.*

The Woman's Story: Waiting

Woman   Everyone knows. They're sitting on the ground staring at the building. The bodies are behind the doors.

They haven't taken them away yet. It takes time. They make us sit and wait. We're all watching. Except the little ones. They're hiding their faces against their mothers. The smoke stings their eyes. Everyone's watching the doors. The hinges are huge iron fists. Inside it's cement. Here there's trees and grass. The last grass I'll touch. It bends like a baby's arm then reaches up again. When the doors open I'll carry you in. You'll never learn to walk. All these people will be dead soon. What's left they scatter on the grass. That's why the earth's grey. Birds hop on it and peck for mites.

The **Mother** *goes out. The* **Woman** *looks towards the* **Boy**.

Woman   Tell me a story. Then my baby will live. (*The* **Boy** *reads*.) You ask me 'what story?' Tell me! You say 'I have to study my book'. Tell me! You say 'will it save all the children?' No. You say 'how will it save yours?' (*She looks towards the doors*.) When they've taken the bodies out they hose the floor. Then they open the doors and push us in.

The **Boy** *closes his book. He lies back and speaks as if to himself.*

Boy   . . . Once there was –

Woman   No no. I told that to the soldiers! A soldier hit my mouth with his rifle. I told the story with blood in my mouth. They pushed me into the lorry.

Boy   Once there was –

Woman   No no I told that too! Think! Try! They've taken the last dead people out. I'm so close to death I know what's happening to them. They're piled outside to be burnt.

Boy   The soldiers have guns! How will a story stop them?

Woman   It only has to stop them for a moment. So that they look down at the stones – for a moment – or look at each other. Then I'll reach up and put my baby in the tree. Where the branches fork – there. Soldiers don't look for babies in trees. They'll think it's rags blown there by the wind. Someone will find it and keep it.

Boy   There's no story!

The **Woman** *goes to the* **Boy**.

Woman Then why did you bring us here? I don't know
you – this house – this room – I don't even know your name.
You brought us here. If you can do that you can tell a story.
My baby will live. When we go in through the doors the
other mothers will cling on to their babies. I won't. I'll put
mine down in a corner. That'll be safe. Away from the feet.
Your story will be in its head! – it'll be too still to die. It goes
so still when it listens! Stiller than a stone. I'll die in another
corner. Then the soldiers won't be suspicious when they look
through the hole – they won't see it. When they take the
bodies out they'll leave it – like a piece of dirt in the corner
when you sweep – you don't bother to sweep it. What else
could they do? Pick it up and knock it against the wall? They
wouldn't! (*To baby*.) The water will save you. They hose the
floor. Your face will be clean in all that filth. When they see it
they'll think of an angel. They'll take you out and keep you.

Boy Why?

Woman They do, they do. People do things to show
they're human! I heard – a soldier – saw a body with a
wristwatch. They'd missed it, hadn't taken it. He bent down
to steal it. The time was wrong. He put it right – and the body
was buried with the watch telling the right time. Even
soldiers have to show themselves they're human! (*Looks
round*.) The people are staring at the door. Their faces are
sad: the terror's in their eyes. Why don't they sing? Hold
hands and dance! It's their world! The soldiers would beat
them with their rifles. (*Turns back to the* **Boy**.) God can't save
it. If he did everyone would know. The world would be
turned upside down. The other mothers would ask why their
child wasn't saved. People would be angry. God dare not
save my child. They'd throw stones at him. The dead
children would spit at him. You can save it. You're nobody.
Nobody knows what you do. Nobody notices. Tell the story!
Perhaps it happens like this all the time! The story's told to
the child – but no one else notices. Not even God. He'd be
ashamed.

Boy   Once there was – once there was –

Woman   It's listening!

Boy   A girl. Her friend had a jumper.

Woman   No no not that! I told it that!

Boy   You can't!

Woman   I have! (*She tells the story, glancing back at the doors of the gas chamber.*)

The Mother's Story: Guilt

Woman   The jumper was bluer than the sky. The girl wanted it. She told her friend to meet her on the street corner. While her friend waited she crept into the house. The jumper was in a drawer. Like a pool of blue blood! (It's not listening! Not listening!) She took it and pressed it to her face. She ran out to the back lane. A stranger came towards her. She realised she could never wear it. People would know it was stolen. She burnt it. It stank. The smoke curled round it like old snakes. She went home. Her mother said what's on your face? (It's not listening!) In the mirror – her face was blue where the jumper had touched it. Her friend had dyed it. Blue. She scrubbed till her face was raw. It wouldn't come off. She scratched with her nails. It wouldn't come off. She cried. Her tears turned blue where they ran in the – The baby's not listening! It's not the story!

Boy   I don't know what story you want!

Woman   Please! They won't let us wait any more! They want to kill us and go home!

The **Boy** *picks up his book and reads.*

Woman   O please – please! Look the man with big boots is coming round the side of the building. He's got the tin of crystals. Gas. He's rattling it. A little boy's put up his hands to play with it. The man's standing at the door. Joking. He doesn't look at us. He doesn't see us.

The **Boy** *closes the book.*

The Boy's Story: Nightmare

Boy   One day the earth got tired of carrying people. They were too heavy. It turned into a ship. No one noticed. They were too busy. A big ship sailing through space. Space was the sea. One day it sank.

Woman   It's listening!

Boy   The people saw the ship was sinking. It pulled them down with it. They reached up and grabbed the clouds. They could reach that far because they were afraid. Everyone in the world hung from the clouds.

Woman   They're giving orders. The man in the boots is easing the lid on the tin with his bayonet. To make sure it's loose.

Boy   The earth sank below them. A great shadow sinking under the sea. It made a deep sigh as it sank till it was gone. The people hung from the clouds. They were so small. Their clothes looked white. They hung upside down like white bats.

A grating sound.

Woman   They're pulling the bolts on the doors.

Boy   They hung day after day. Then an old man fell into the empty space. More fell. They vanished. Sometimes whole flocks broke away and fell together like the side of a cliff.

Woman   The man in boots is climbing the ladder.

Boy   In the end there were only a few left. Little white shapes hanging from the clouds. They didn't speak. They had to keep their strength.

Woman   He's taking the tin up to the roof.

Boy   Then only one was hanging. The rest had fallen. It was a child and it couldn't speak.

*The book falls from the **Boy**'s hand.*

Woman   That's not the story! It didn't listen! Quickly!
Tell me –

Metallic sounds. People begin to cry and call.

What's that? – the terrible squeaking? The dead are crying!
No – the hinges! They're opening the doors. (*To baby.*) Wait,
wait – it takes ten minutes – twenty! All that time! Something
will save you! – The people are getting to their feet.
Stumbling. The doors are open. The great wet mouth. Water
dripping from the top like saliva. (*An old woman wailing.*) An
old woman beating her neighbours. Beating. Kicking. The
soldiers are beating – dragging! The soldiers are screaming
as if *they're* going to die! The poor people sobbing. My
precious I'll shield you. Not one mark. Bruise. Scratch. I
won't let death touch you.

She bends over the baby to protect it.

That is it. That is it. You walk into it. That is how it is.

She walks into the gas chamber.

Three

*The **Boy** lies awake on the bed. The **Mother** is heard from another
room.*

Mother   Whoopppeeee! Luvvy! Luvvy!

*Pause. The **Mother** runs in.*

We passed! We passed! (*She waves an envelope and three slips of
paper.*) I opened the envelope! We passed!

*The **Boy** jumps from the bed. He grabs for the papers. The **Mother**
dances away with them. The **Boy** chases her, grabbing.*

Mother   We passed! We passed!

Boy   Yippeee! I passed! I passed! Show me! Let me –

*The **Boy** gets one of the slips. Reads it.*

Boy   Maths B!

Mother   Good! Good!

Boy (*gets the other slips. Reads*)   Science double A!

Mother   Double A! Science!

Boy   History – agh! (*Stops in disappointment.*) They didn't mark it right! – German B!

Mother (*looking at the history result*)   What's it mean?

Boy (*reads*)   English A! English lit A!

Mother   We passed in English! We passed!

Boy   Art B!

Woman (*off – screams*)

Mother   We deserved it! We worked! I don't begrudge the overtime! I'll phone Mrs Lacey – she's on late turn this week. I hope her Ron hasn't let her down. You're good lads! Don't stand there! Aren't you pleased? I'm more excited than you! Enjoy it!

Woman (*off*)   My baby! My baby! People – so many! I've lost it! My baby my baby my baby!

Mother   Luvvy? – O dear I shouldn't have opened the envelope. I couldn't wait. I thought it was bad news. I wanted to prepare you. Luvvy – don't. You stood like that last time. Don't upset me today. Sit down. Be a good boy. It was my fault running up the stairs. I know what you're like. Is it the history? You got four As! Don't spoil it for me. I can't afford to be ill like you. If I let go I'd never get back. I have to fight. I use my fists. Now I can't even enjoy this. Everything I have gets broken. Like that cup.

The **Woman** *comes in without the baby. The* **Boy** *covers his face with one hand.*

Woman   Give me my baby!

Boy   You – I remember you from? – the street? –

Mother (*staring at the* **Boy**)   What is it? O God I wish I'd never heard of exams! If I knew what it'd mean I'd've stopped you doing them!

Woman Help me. My baby is in there. All the people. They'll crush it. I tried to put it in a corner. I couldn't. The feet, the feet! (*Turns to look back and call.*) Don't hurt my baby! (*To the* **Boy**.) I had it. Suddenly it was gone. My hands were empty. The people were like a river dragging it away. (*Turns and shouts.*) Don't kill my baby! I'll curse you when I'm dead! (*To the* **Boy**.) Help me!

Mother (*to the* **Boy**)   Why must you punish me?

The **Mother** *goes.*

Woman Quick! (*Gestures.*) In there! They're going to die! My baby's in there! It might as well be thrown in a machine! Someone's picked it up for hers. Kissing and hugging it. My baby wants *me*! Not her! Don't let it die like this! Find it! Look they're crushed against the doors where they'll be dragged out when they're dead! Poor people, poor people! (*Calls.*) My baby – my baby! (*To the* **Boy**.) You're afraid! They went in. Thousands went in. Thousands and thousands. The steps are worn by bare feet. It's their shrine. Their holy place. They won't come back! You can! You can go in and out! You're not going to die. I wasted so much time! – asking for stories! As if they'd help *here*! Go in! My arms are empty. Don't let me die like this. I didn't know it would be like this. Let me die with my baby. I won't ask for anything else. Only that.

The **Woman** *takes the* **Boy**'s *hand. They go into the gas chamber. The sounds of a railway terminus – a few voices calling, bangs and metallic squeaks and clangs. They continue as the* **Boy** *and* **Woman** *speak.*

Woman (*to the* **Boy**)   Here. Inside. Don't be afraid.

Boy So many people.

Woman A whirlpool of flesh and bones. Don't look at them. You can't help. Look for something small. Still. Don't give me another woman's. Only simple things now. I can't suffer any more. I'd go mad.

The sounds of the very old woman in hysteria.

Don't look at her. It's the old woman. She was beating her neighbours outside.

The **Boy** *picks up the baby from the bed.*

Boy   This –

Woman   Mine? Mine? Look! Be sure! You know it!

Boy   Yes.

He gives the baby to the **Woman**. *He starts to go.*

I can't do any more.

Woman   Tell me the story.

Boy   There is no story!

Woman   Tell me!

Boy   You told a story to the soldiers! It didn't stop them!

Woman   They wouldn't listen!

Boy   They won't listen here! It's going to die! You're all going to die! You're dead already! I can't save you!

Woman   Tell it the story!

The sound of the doors closing.

They're closing the doors! Quick! Tell it! If you don't you'll never forget this! Never! Tell it for *your* sake!

The **People**'*s groans and cries continue and grow louder, more desperate.*

People   Help us! Help us!

A noise from the roof – stamping, harsh scraping.

Boy   What's that? Up there! A giant on the roof!

Woman   The man in boots. He climbed the ladder. He's got the gas! Tell the story! Quick! Help the people!

People   What story? The man knows the story! What man?

Woman (*calls*)   If he tells the story my baby won't die!

People   The baby won't die! We won't die! The man knows the story! Tell us! The story! The story!

Boy   Look! Up there! A star! No a hole in the roof! Light coming through the –! He's opened a hole in the roof!

Woman   Please! – it'll be too late!

The sounds on the roof turn to thunder. The **People** *are groaning and calling.*

Boy   Thunder!

Woman   The man on the roof! His boots are like thunder because we're going to die!

Boy   The hole's gone dark! The man's looking in! His shadow! His eye glaring at us!

Woman   He's opening the can!

People   The story! The story!

Woman   Tell it! Tell it!

The rushing sound of a giant hailstorm.

Boy   Rain – dust – pouring – what! – broken glass – pouring from the hole!

Woman   The crystals! He's emptying the can! Tell the story – now! That's why you're here! You came to tell it!

Boy   No! I can't stop it! It's too late! It was long ago!

People   The story! The story!

Thunder.

Woman   The lid clattering on the roof!

People (*groaning, choking*)   Help us! Story! Story!

Man on Roof (*huge laugh*)   I'm the man on the roof! Burning human rubbish! Let 'em eat it!

People   Help us!

Boy (*suddenly points at* **Woman**)   You! It's you! Blame her! – blame her! Years ago – when you were here – dying! – you told it a story! You nursed it – here! You wanted to be a mother – here! You told it a story – here!

Woman (*choking*)   I did. I should've screamed. Held it up for them to see. Show the snot pouring from its face. I should've strangled it. Thrown it at them – dead! A dead nothing they can't hurt! But I told it a story. And someone – dying next to me – listened – put out his hand and touched my child – its head – a blessing – we choked to death – I didn't finish. Finish it for the child –

The **Boy** *takes the child. The thunder and groans go on. The* **Man on Roof** *laughs.*

Boy   The man didn't bless it – he wanted something to hold on to! You told it a story – while dead people were leaning on you! (*Looks up.*) A hole in the sky. A face in the hole. Emptying a tin of gas – It's my baby! I'll take it away. And nothing can go on. It'll stop. All this – stop. You'll stay here like this for ever. Like breath trapped in a hole in an iceberg.

Silence.

Slowly the faint murmur of voices trapped in time begins.

People   . . . it's my throat . . . cutting . . . blind . . . my bones are breaking . . .

Woman   You can't keep them here for ever . . . ! – (*Calls.*) Poor people, my child didn't want you to suffer this . . . Give me the child. Let them die.

Boy   No.

Woman   Give me the child.

Boy   I can't.

Woman   You must. My baby must die. With us. You make its pain last: I can feel its fingers clenching –

Boy   I can't let it die.

Woman   It can die here – it doesn't matter here – no one will notice – it won't make enough ash to tread in –

People   . . . my belly's a fire . . . the knife's dancing in my throat . . .

Isolated distorted thunderclaps: the **Man on Roof** *is crying.*

Man on Roof Help me! I'm on the roof! Crouched at the hole. Pouring the tin. The tin can't empty. The crystals are pouring. Through the hole. Falling on their shoulders. In their hair. They never stop. I can't move from the hole. It's screwed on my face like a mask. The dying are looking at me. Not in hate. In surprise. I've killed thousands. Thousands. The crystals are pouring. The tin won't empty. Don't look at me! Don't make me stay here for ever! Don't make me kill any more! Let me go away! Help me! Tell me a story!

People . . . let us die . . .

Woman (*choking*) My throat's turning to ribbons.

Man on Roof (*anger*) Don't look at me! You used to topple over! I saw your arses swimming in the filth!

Thunder, rushing hail.

The crystals are pouring – they're sand in an hourglass – but time doesn't pass! (*Crying.*) Help me! Pity me! I want a story!

Boy (*to baby*) You won't die. I promise you.

*The **Boy** goes out with the baby.*

People (*groans*) . . . story . . . story . . . story . . .

Woman (*choking*) Tell the story –

Four

*The **Mother** lies exhausted and half-asleep on the **Boy**'s bed. She holds the exam-result slips. Suddenly she starts up.*

Mother (*calls*) That you? I've been worried sick. Where've you been? I sent for the doctor. Then I had to put him off. They were really nasty. Said there was nothing wrong with you if you could walk the streets.

She sits on the side of the bed.

*A very **Old Woman** comes in. Her hair is beautiful and white and flows down to her knees. She wears an old, loose-fitting white smock and a comfortable old straw hat – half-way between a boater and a sunhat.*

*The rim is a little dented and frayed and is decorated with an artificial
flower. Her face looks like a linen mask.*

Mother   I thought it was my son. I heard the door.

Old Woman   No, me.

Mother   I'm worried sick.

Old Woman   Your son's all right. He'll be here soon.
Don't be angry with him. All young people want to change
the world. Get an idea and can't let it go. He went for a walk.

Mother   He's all right?

Old Woman   Yes. He's growing up. You must let him be.

Mother   I look after him. He gets his meals. I work. What
more can I do? He gets the same clothes as his mates.

Old Woman   Yes, that too.

Mother   Who are you?

Old Woman   I came to tell you your son's safe.

The **Boy** *comes in carrying the baby.*

Old Woman (*little giggle*)   You're in trouble. Your
mother'll give it to you now!

Mother   Where've you been? I had to put the doctor off.
The receptionist was really spiteful! What's that?

Boy   A baby.

Mother   A baby? Whose?

Boy   They were going to kill it.

The **Old Woman** *goes to the baby and looks at it. She makes a sound
of contempt and turns away.*

Boy   If I told it a story it'd live.

Old Woman   Wouldn't waste a story on that. Mucky little
tyke. Throw it away.

Mother   You can't keep someone's baby.

Boy   People were being killed.

Old Woman   How?

Boy   There was a man on a roof.

Old Woman   A man on a roof? How'd he get up there?

Boy   Up a ladder.

Old Woman (*laughs*)   A ladder? Up a ladder?

Boy   Yes.

Old Woman (*laughs*)   He climbed a ladder to kill people?

Boy   He had a tin of crystals.

Old Woman (*laughs*)   A tin? He had a tin of – crystals! (*Laughs.*)

Boy   She doesn't believe me. I saw it.

The **Old Woman**'s *laughter is free and joyful.*

Old Woman   O I believe you! It's so funny! (*Laughs.*)

Boy   They killed people! Thousands. Thousands. They burnt them!

Old Woman (*laughs*)   Thousands – th- th- thousands! (*Laughs.*) It's funny funny funny! Thousands and th- th- thousands. Burnt! (*Laughs.*)

Boy   They were screaming!

Old Woman (*explodes with laughter*)   Screaming! Thousands and thousands! Screaming! Thousands and th- th- ! O it's funny funny funny!

Boy   She's mad! – They killed them while they were burning people they'd already killed!

Old Woman (*laughs*)   Already killed! Already killed! O stop him! Funny funny funny! (*Wipes her eyes.*) O stop him! Burnt! – already killed – already k- k- k- killed!

Boy (*to* **Mother**)   In a concrete room. Their faces – they were like animals who knew they were in a slaughterhouse.

Old Woman (*suddenly explodes with laughter*)   Animals! Slaughterhouse! – knew they were in a – O stop him! (*Wipes her eyes. Laughs.*) A man on a ladder – funny funny –

Boy   I saw it! He had boots on!

Old Woman (*shrieks with laughter*)   Boots! He had boots! A tin! On a l- l- l- l- – . O stop him stop him stop him! It hurts! Boots! (*Screams with laughter, then suppresses it.*) What – what – just tell me – what did he do with the – what did the man on the roof with the – the boots and ladder – do with the *tin*! (*She explodes with laughter.*)

Boy   He emptied it in the hole.

Old Woman (*roaring with laughter*)   Emptied it in the – ! The hole! (*Rocks with laughter.*) Emptied it in the – ! He – he – he – had a hole in the roof! (*Trying to control herself.*) O he's a good boy! He means well. He means – . (*Bursts out laughing.*) On a ladder! A ladder!

Boy   They were in pain!

Old Woman (*laughs*)   Pain! Pain! Pain! (*Tries to control herself.*) Yes yes, yes yes. (*Laughs.*) Pain! P- p- p-. (*Laughing, gestures to the baby.*) Throw it away. Stands there with his doll. I've seen funnier things than your man on a l- l- l-. I saw a whole city. (*Laughing joyfully.*) One morning. Birds singing. Bicycle bells ringing. People off to work. Off to school. Waving goodbye. (*Laughs.*) They never saw each other again. All the faces clean and white. All morning washed. Like china still in the factory. Something came floating down the sky. A moment after: all the faces were black. White – black! (*Laughs.*) Suddenly! – like a rabbit from a hat. No one knew who they were talking to! They all looked the same! Scorched! Black! (*Laughs.*) The clothes didn't tell them – *they* were black. Burnt! (*Laughs.*)

Boy   Tell me the story.

Old Woman (*laughs*)   Me?

Boy   You know it.

Old Woman   Why does he say that?

Boy You laugh because you know it. Tell the child and it'll grow up.

Old Woman (*laughs*) Once I saw – No that makes me laugh too much. Talk about something else. Talk about – (*Begins again.*) Once I saw – (*Laughs.*) this is funny – once I saw a tower. On top of a green hill. They pushed people in it. Locked the door. Put wood and bracken round it. Set it on fire! (*Laughs louder.*) Wait! – this is the funny bit! The tower didn't burn! It was good solid stone. So the tower was like an oven! The people inside roasted! (*Laughs.*) Imagine! – the tower was an oven to roast – roast people! Imagine! (*Laughing.*) All the grass on the hill turned black. The people outside dancing and rolling in the grass. The dancing people were as black as the roasted people. (*Laughs.*)

Boy Who is she?

Mother She came to tell me you were all right.

Old Woman (*laughing happily*) One of my best times was at a drowning. Like a regatta! Top people in pretty hats. Raised their glasses to the waves. They were important people, toffs – they had music! Then they threw the captives in the river. Splash! The young men held them under with oars! The musicians scraped away! (*Laughs.*) The fish swam off! (*Laughs.*)

Boy D'you laugh at everything?

Old Woman (*laughing*) I do. I love to laugh. I laugh at people. The funny things they do. (*Explosion of laughter.*) A man in boots climbs a ladder with a tin – and – (*Stomps to imitate climbing a ladder. Howls with laughter.*) He said it! Don't deny it! You saw it! (*Laughs.*) – he emptied it in the hole! (*Laughs.*)

Boy There's something you can't laugh at.

Old Woman (*explodes with laughter*) Something I can't – something I can't –! O that's funny! Funny funny funny! O he makes me laugh!

Boy The baby's face.

The **Boy** *gives the* **Old Woman** *the baby.*

Old Woman (*stares at the baby. Bursts into laughter*)   It's hungry! Hungry! O hunger's so funny! Hungry babies best! So funny funny funny. Look – all the hunger in the world in its little empty mouth! Little empty fists grab-grabbing up there! That won't do any good! (*Points a finger at the sky.*) It's empty up there! Fat ickle-lickle empty tum-tum! (*Laughs.*) O hungry babies are a scream! So funny! (*To the* **Boy**.) Take your little toy – here, take it. (*Chuckling happily.*) Once I saw – I'll tell you – you're a good boy: an empty house – the broken windows – plaster ceilings on the floor – a little baby crawling through the empty rooms. Till it comes to the bone. It sucks the bone. (*Imitates.*) Minch – minch – minch – like babies do. (*Laughs.*) The bone was once in its mother. It ate its mother's bone. (*Laughs.*)

Boy (*reaching for the baby*)   You're mad! Some poor old mad woman! You see nothing! Nothing!

Old Woman   Nothing!

The **Old Woman** *lifts her smock: underneath a dress, filthy, bloody, torn, scorched, soot-marked, foul with corruption.*

Old Woman   Nothing? And this? This is nothing? I walk among the dead and dying! I wipe tears still wet from the dead faces – with this! I mop blood from wounds. I drag it through the ruins. I wear it next to my skin. I see nothing? (*Laughs.*) Look! (*Points to a stain.*) – tears from an old mother mourning her butchered grandchildren. Here's a woman driven mad with suffering – she ripped it with her teeth. This is chips of flesh from a slaughter pit. Tanks drove over there. The powder-burns from shells stencilled the skeletons. This is special, this bit: soot from the city that burned black one morning. You saw a room of dying people? (*Laughs.*) I see more pain in the cracked face of a doll than you see in your baby! I'm wise in pain and sin! (*Holds out the baby.*) Take it! Your little bit of flesh! Take it and throw it away with the rest!

The **Boy** *takes the baby.*

Old Woman (*laughs*)   A man on a ladder! With a tin! And boots! A ladder! . . . (*Quietens.*) When I fall to sleep the children come to play on my dress. They trace the patterns with their little fingers. They draw the pictures you can draw in fire and water too. My children love my dress. When they grow up they want to be married in it – and dress their children in it to be named. (*Laughs.*) Touch it. Touch my dress. The blind old sages read this braille. He tells me what *he's* seen! (*Points.*) Touch it! Touch *this* – that blood hates the man who shed it. Still rails and curses him all night. My dress is full of voices. They groan like a forest falling from the sky. The children play a game on it. They throw the dice and move their stones from crime to crime. Well. You've seen enough. Down dress. The curtain's closed.

She lowers the smock over the dress. Silence.

(*To the* **Boy**.) You mend your manners. Throw that brat away for a start! If it grew up and you told it about its mother it wouldn't want to live. (*Laughs.*) It'd kill itself. I haven't laughed so much in years.

Boy   Tell me the story.

Old Woman   Story, story! If I told you the story you wouldn't understand. And anyway, I don't know it. All the people on my dress gossip. The dead love to gossip. I listen to that. It makes me laugh. One little girl (*She taps her dress.*) – had every bone in her body broken – yes, every one – and when her mother picked her up – she hung from her hand as limp as a wet floorcloth – sopping. The mother goes on and on about it. The others shut her up. They all want to gossip. A lot of good it does them! I know everything except the story. (*She giggles a little.*) I can't know that. (*Gestures to the* **Mother**.) She knows. That stupid lump. The story's been living with you all the time. Only she's forgot it.

Boy (*to* **Mother**)   Remember. Please.

Mother   It's please now.

Boy   Take the baby. It'll remind you.

Mother   I can't.

Boy   Please.

Mother   You always want. It's always something. Why should I do more? I'm your skivvy. I have no pleasure. What d'you give me?

Boy   Look at it.

Mother   Throw it away. She's right. This is my house. I don't want it here. Get rid of it.

Boy   It's my place too.

Mother   And you! You go with it! I don't want you. Leave me alone. Leave me in peace. Want want want! I could've – when they're little it's easy – left you on a bus. Made sure there was nothing to lead them to me. I thought of it. I could've killed you. Don't think it doesn't happen. Then I'd've had a life. Not wasted it. Had my pleasure like other women.

Boy   Look at it!

Mother   No. I don't want to go through all that again.

Old Woman (*half absent-mindedly*)   There was a boy running in a field. A man flew over in a plane. He fired his machine gun. The dust kicked up behind the boy. The airman drove him on with his bullets. The dust flew behind his heels. (*Laughs.*) Just before he reached the trees the airman shot him. When he fell, guess what that clever boy did? He cartwheeled.

*The **Boy** forces the baby into the **Mother**'s hands.*

Boy   Look at it!

Mother   No no no no!

*The **Mother** looks at the baby.*

Boy   Its face!

Mother   I was looking at its hands to see if it was alive. A dead baby's hands let go. Open. Is that its face? It's like a knot tied in rope and trodden on. Its hands are old . . .

Boy Think! Anything! The story'll come!

Mother There are all sorts of stories. Who can tell?

Boy Begin – I'll remember it.

Mother Once there was – no.

She stops. She can't remember. She gives the baby to the **Boy***. Silence.*

There was always suffering. Children lost. Wicked queens. Mad dragons. The giant was always hungry. (*Pause.*) The beast they hunted in the wood and shot it with an arrow – through the heart. It had to be a golden arrow. It had to be the heart. The beast – its mangy, dirty hide – turned into a prince. When the king saw his son he embraced him. He fell on his neck and wept. And when the courtiers pulled out the arrow he died. And the old king wept. I can't remember.

The **Mother** *goes to the* **Old Woman***. She crouches at her feet like a child. The* **Old Woman** *hides her under her smock.*

Old Woman (*patting the* **Mother***'s head under the smock*) There was always suffering.

Mother (*under the smock*) The tears. This is the burnt house. This is the soldiers cut to pieces in the trenches. This is the sailors lost at sea. This is the hungry waiting with empty plates. These are the stones. There isn't a story. They're all mixed together. That's why I love my son – that's why I love you luvvy. Forgive me. You're all I have.

Old Woman (*resting her hand on the smock over the* **Mother***'s head*) People blown up like a jigsaw. You can't put them together.

Boy (*to the* **Old Woman**) You know the story. You're so old you forgot it and remembered it lots of times. Remember it now.

Old Woman Ah – he thinks I'm old! That's it.

She uncovers the **Mother** *and moves away. The* **Mother** *stays crouched on the ground with her face in her knees. The* **Old Woman** *goes towards the door.*

I must go. (*Stops.*) This house'll be dust. The street outside, dust. You'll go too – like the little clutch of clinker – human clinker – in your hands. Don't go too soon. Why rush? Wait your turn. (*Gestures round.*) All this, all this, there was no need. It didn't have to be. People blown in the wind. The storm. No need. (*Starts to go. Stops.*) He thinks I'm old. I'm not yet born. One day I will be. One day I'll live on this earth. A long time will pass till then. That scrap in your hands'll be ancient, ancient, ancient when I'm born – so old ashes'll be green. (*Lifts the smock a little, peers at it.*) My eyes are going. What is . . . ? It itches. (*Looks up.*) In my dress there's a pocket deeper than the grave. It must be. Those who suffered most sleep in it. They don't want to wake and tell. All they want is silence. To sleep for ever. My laughing disturbs them. They're stirring. Hush, hush. (*Wearily walks away.*) When it's gone – all of it – I'll be born . . . No need, no need. I wear it next to my skin.

The **Mother** *stands and follows the* **Old Woman** *out.*

Boy (*looks at the baby*)   You were killed before I was born. What can I do? Take you back to die.

The **Boy** *goes out with the baby.*

Five

The **Woman** *and the* **People** *groaning, the* **Man on Roof** *crying. One continuous sound stuck in time.*

The **Boy** *comes in with the baby.*

Woman (*choking*)   Look – the people – air stuck in their throats like a stone – can't breathe in or out – the dying can move, *they* can't – cruel cruel – too late to help – you came too late –

Boy   I wanted the child to live.

Woman   I carried it here. I knew what happens in the end. I told it a story – in this misery – filth! What else? Was it wrong? Is the concrete angry? Did I insult it by being human in front of it? I told it a story without hope. I didn't know you could tell a story without hope. (*She takes the baby from the* **Boy**.) I stood here. Held it like this. I said – once there was a poor man. He walked in the forest. The forest was dark. I couldn't finish. I died. I dropped my baby. It was kicked. Trodden on. I saw the naked feet and the concrete. My baby spinning like a wheel. Finish the story! It must be told! In this place! Here!

Boy Once there was –

Woman Yes, once – once there was –

Boy A poor man. Who walked in the forest. The forest was dark –

The **People** *begin to cry in new pain.*

Woman Look! Look! It's a spell! The people are moving! Tell it! Finish it! We can die again! We can die!

Boy In the darkness there was a hut.

Woman In the darkness there was a hut.

The **People**'*s groaning and crying is growing louder.*

Man on Roof The tin! It's emptying! Yippee! It's scattering like lice! They've got it all! Let 'em eat it!

Boy And in the hut – and in the hut – I can't! – I can't! –

Woman And in the hut – was music –

Man on Roof This lot won't take long! Look at 'em tumble!

The groaning, gasping and crying goes on.

People Ah! Ah! Ah! Ah!

Woman (*choking*) In the hut was music – singing – in the hut – he tried – grope to the hut – in the dark – trees – in his way –

Man on Roof Eat it up my luvvies! Don't waste the din-dins!

Woman Try! Try!

Boy   I can't!

Woman   Try! The trees were bigger – trees – branches – arms pulling him – legs kicking – trees – crushing – baby baby –

People (*screaming, groaning, raving*) Ah! Ah! Ah! Ah!

Man on Roof   Look at 'em tumble! What a circus. (*Shout of laughter.*) One's standing on his head!

Woman   Take – take – (*She reaches the baby to the* **Boy**.) Tell it – !

Boy   I can't! I can't – ! It happened long ago! It's over!

Thunder: the **Man on Roof** *dancing in his boots and clapping his hands in time with his steps.*

Man on Roof   Tumbling! Dancing! Clowns!

The **People***'s groaning and screaming are more desperate.*

Woman (*reaching the baby to the* **Boy**)   Take it! – tell – tell it – the story!

The **Boy** *takes the bundle. The groaning and screaming is uglier.*

Woman   Naked feet – stamping – kicking!

Boy   Singing – there – the man heard singing in the hut – singing –

Man on Roof   This beats the lot! They're telling stories!

Groans. Screams. Thunder. Dancing boots. The **Man on Roof** *laughs. The* **Woman** *falls. Blind. She gropes for the baby.*

Boy   Singing – singing –

Woman (*reaching for the baby*)   Touch it – touch – touch my – last – last –

The **Woman** *reaches up. Half-dead. Pulls at the bundle. It unwraps into a sheet. It falls on the* **Boy**. *Covers him. He falls. Cringes under the sheet.*

Man on Roof   Tumblers!

Thunder. Groans. Screams.

Boy (*under the sheet, rolling on the ground*)   Trees were holding
– crushing – back – the man – he heard it – singing – in the –
hut – singing – in the – singing – singing –

The **Woman**'s *spasms stop. She is dead. A strange new sound begins.
At first it is hardly heard in the uproar. Slowly it grows louder: the
groans and screams are changing into the sound of the* **People**'s *breath
– and all their breathing is joined together into one breath. The sound of
a crowd of sleepers breathing together as one.*

Boy   What is – what is – ?

*The shared, common breath grows louder – rising and falling in the
shape of a wave – the other sounds die away under it: till the only sound
heard is the people breathing together as one. The sound is neither
beautiful nor ugly.*

The people. All the – together. Breathing. Together. Dying.
Breathing.

The sound dies away into silence. The **People** *are dead. The* **Boy** *is
sitting on the ground, wrapped in the sheet, his head sticking from the
top.*

Finished. The man's down from the roof. Quiet even outside.
Something stamping. Horse's hoof. Sometimes they cart the
dead away in horse-and-carts. The doors.

The doors open: cold light falls across the **Boy**. *He sits huddled under
the sheet. His head is bare.*

Light falling on the bodies. Heap of wreckage out of the sea.
Small. I didn't know people were so small. Death's made
them white. (*Looks up.*) Men in the doorway. Shadows with
chains and hooks. Coming to take the bodies.

The **Boy** *stands. He drags the* **Woman** *towards the men, the sheet
trailing behind him.*

Six

The **Mother** *slouched on the bed. She stares in front of her. She is deep
in thought.*

The **Boy** *comes in.*

Mother   Where've you been?

Boy   For a walk?

Mother   Again? In the dark?

Boy   It's all right.

Mother   Where d'you walk in the dark?

Boy   I'm not a child.

Mother   While you're under my roof you live by the rules. You tell me what you get up to. It's for your own good. I'm tired. I suppose you're off out celebrating with your mates this evening?

The Story

Boy   Once. A man walking in a dark forest. A hut in the distance. He heard singing from the hut. Happy. Beautiful. He went towards it. Hard. Bushes and trees in the way. He came to the hut. He stopped outside the door. He listened. It was late. He was hungry and tired. He knocked. The singing stopped. The door was unlocked. He opened it and went in. The hut was empty. No fire in the grate. No candle. The shelves were bare. A cup and plate on the table. They were empty. The cup was wet. There were crumbs by the plate. He left the hut and went on. Before he'd gone far the singing in the hut started again. He didn't turn back. He knew what'd happen if he did. After that, starting from that day, whenever he met someone in the forest sick or old or wounded or in need he –

Mother   I'm working late tonight. You'll have to look after yourself. Food in the fridge. Someone has to make up the money.

Pause.

Boy   I made some tea.

Notes and Commentary

Roads to the Inland Sea

Boy   The soldiers have guns! How will a story stop them?

Woman   It only has to stop them for a moment. So that they
look down at the stones – for a moment – or look at each other.

In February 1995, a small theatre company in Birmingham, working
in a theatre form with minimal national profile and under severe
economic threat, persuaded one of Europe's most respected and con-
troversial playwrights to write them a new play. By September,
Edward Bond's *At the Inland Sea* was in rehearsal with Big Brum
Theatre-in-Education company and from 16 October to 14
December it toured to schools and colleges in the West Midlands.
These notes tell two stories. One is of that particular production, the
other is the story of a writer and a theatre form – Theatre-in-Education
– moving inexorably together to share artistic and political objectives
and finally, in 1995, collaborating directly.

At the Inland Sea – Telling a Radical Story

When Bond agreed to write a play for young people, it was almost
inevitable that the idea of the Imagination would in some way be at
its heart. It has been a constant theme in his entire output. When a
gang of young men murder a baby in a London park (*Saved*, 1965),
their inhibitions are lowered because they can't imagine themselves as
other than isolated individuals. Like the baby, who is dosed with
aspirin, they are semi-conscious imaginatively. They take their cue
from a culture that meets with contempt and neglect their instinctive
demands for a fullness of life. In 1965 this seemed outrageous to some,
and the state censor banned the play. It *is* outrageous of course, but at
least no one can now claim that such atrocities are exaggerated. They
happen in parks, by railway lines, in front of schools, in suburban front-
rooms. Bond's *Bingo* (1971) interrogates the single individual William
Shakespeare, that icon of the power of imagination, about his actions
as a landowner in such a way as to cast doubt on the great writer's own-
ership of his own imagination. When he fails to resist the land enclo-
sures that will pauperize local people near his Stratford home, the
imagination that created Lear on the heath can't cope with the contradiction. A dreadful truth has to be faced:

> I spent so much of my youth, my best energy . . . for this: New
> Place. Somewhere to be sane in. It was all a mistake. There's a

taste of bitterness in my mouth . . . I howled when they suffered, but they were whipped and hanged so that I could be free.

In his 'Rough Notes on Theatre', Bond writes this about the organic relationship between Imagination and Story:

Imagination is essentially storyable. Imagination needs to relate experience as story or as potentially storyable. When experience becomes overwhelming or chaotic, radical stories are told.

Once the common ground of the Imagination had been agreed between Bond and Big Brum, a web of connections was opened up between the subject and the medium they were working in. Theatre, after all, is nothing more (*and nothing less*) than telling stories, and the human imagination is the driving force of story. It makes the structures of story organic, malleable and usable. On a very basic level, the imagination would have developed as an evolutionary tool favouring 'primitive' people who predicted the outcome of their actions, rather than left them to chance. The ability to predict what would happen if seeds were sewn in moist as opposed to dry soil (the ability to imagine the outcome) was well rewarded by Natural Selection. Imaginers prospered, where those stuck only in the moment died out. And as the imaginers gained control over their imaginative power, so would have begun a feeling understanding of what it meant to hurt another human being. Morality can't function without imagination to allow us to project ourselves feelingly into the experience of others. Morality, therefore, has nothing to do with the control of our behaviour (whether by ourselves or by our betters), but everything to do with the free activity of uncorrupted imagination.

Once there was a . . .[1]

*

Once there was a boy who spent days and nights working hard in his room. He knew that he had to work hard to be able to live well in the big world outside. His mother wanted him to do well and he wanted to please her.

One night, while the boy was studying hard in his room, it seemed that suddenly a strange woman appeared, a woman he had never seen before, except perhaps in pictures. She wore old, ragged clothes and she carried a bundle of rags. Inside the bundle, the boy could just see a tiny baby.

The woman looked frightened and asked the boy to help her. She told the boy that she was going to be taken to a cave, where a man in boots would kill her and her baby. She said that this giant would sprinkle crystals on her head, and on her baby, and then he would eat them both. Only a story, she said, could stop this terrible thing from happening. But it had to be a very special story . . .

*

---

[1] The italicized story is mine written as a commentary on the play – T.C.

A summary of the play's action is deceptively simple. A teenage boy, living with his mother, revises for his History exams in his bedroom. As he works, a woman from the past materializes in his room. Over the course of the play the boy is taken on an imaginative journey during which he is forced to confront her immediate need — to save herself and her baby from being herded into a gas chamber at Auschwitz. By the play's end, the mother and her son have been profoundly changed by the experience. So on one level the play is about the horror of the concentration camps, and of the bureaucratic–industrial system that ran them. It has to be acknowledged that there are young people for whom the facts of Nazism are only dimly known, if known at all. As generations accumulate between the present and the events of the 1930s and 40s, the stark information has to live increasingly in stories — in books, films, art — as indirect testimony rather than as terrible memory. *At the Inland Sea* is, then, another act of witness that uses drama to keep the wound of the extermination camps open and its pain unavoidable. It is one of the play's achievements that it uses language and imagery of great concreteness to bring its audience, in imagination, not only to the iron door of the gas chamber but inside its cement walls. What could be a purely negative experience for the audience is transformed into one of exceptional concentration and engagement because the performance style created by the writing continually emphasizes the *theatre* we are witnessing. The gas chamber is in our mind. What we see is an actor in a stage set that consists mainly of a bed and a chair. What we *know* is a little of what it means to die in a gas chamber.

So *At the Inland Sea* also performs an exciting act of synthesis. The play is *about* Imagination, and its absolute centrality to the state of being human, but it also sets out consciously to create the very imaginative power in its audience that is its subject matter — Imagination is its subject but it is also the means for interacting with the play. Bond links the importance of Imagination to being human by showing it working in the transition from childhood to adulthood. The cliché has it that children are our future. Bond emphasizes that there is an active component — that the young *make* the future, consciously or not. They are, in his phrase, Agents of the Future. For the Big Brum production, he set out the broad aims and scope of the script he had written:

As young people grow, they enter a crisis
It is the unavoidable crisis of the imagination
In this crisis, imagination and reality collide
In the collision, young people pass from childhood to adulthood
They choose how they will live
If reality destroys the imagination, then however busy and
    eminent they become, they will always be empty, a cause of loss

and suffering to others
If the crisis is solved well, if imagination and reality are joined,
    they will live creatively
The crisis is not a rite of passage – such a rite may mark only the
    entry into an existing order of things, natural and social
But in the crises we become either creators of our world – or in one
    way or another, in fact in many ways, its destroyers
Our society does not understand this crisis
Often it does not even notice it or have time and patience for it
Often it is not even noticed by the young people themselves – to
    them it may be a confusion to be brushed aside
They do not know they are choosing how they will live, and –
    together – deciding the future of our communities
The crisis becomes even more important in a changing world
    where new choices will have to be made

The play argues that it is not our intellect or skills that make us
human. We are made human by imagination. In the crisis the
imagination must create a threefold map of past, present and
future. We live on this map. Without it we pass our life lost in an
unmapped 'nobody's' land. The play begins with a young student
in a bedroom. The student prepares to go to school. It is exam day.
A stranger enters the bedroom. There is danger outside. Soldiers
are in the streets. The stranger makes a request that seems strange
and useless . . .

In the spring of 1995, Bond began the process of note-making that gave
birth to the play. On the surface, these notes are an apparently random
brainstorming of ideas, perceptions, analyses, and images, though
closer inspection reveals them as more like a web – intricate and
tough, connecting ideas with images, testing and recombining both in
a laboratory for the writing of the play. As time goes on, there is also an
increasing number of what are recognizably 'play ideas' – scraps of
plot, character ideas, visual images – that slowly transform into the
images of the play as finally written. To sink into these unpublished
notes is to appreciate the degree to which Bond allows his imagination
and his rationality not just to coexist but to feed off each other. In fact
there is no artificial barrier in these notes between the insights of feeling
and those of analysis. As the psychiatrist and – potently for the material
of *At the Inland Sea* – survivor of Dachau and Buchenwald, Bruno Bettelheim, wrote:

No longer can we be satisfied with a life where the heart has its
reasons which reason cannot know. Our hearts must know the
world of reason, and reason must be guided by an informed heart.

The period of winter 1994 through to spring 1995 was notable for news of some of the cruellest atrocities of the Yugoslavian Civil War. It was not possible for a writer like Bond, whose personal and artistic animus against violence is so strong, to be unaffected by these events, sanitized and censored though they mostly were by TV news. Reports in some sections of the press were able to convey more of the true horror of what was happening, including the first images of concentration camps and descriptions of mass murder in Europe since the end of the Second World War. The play's image of the woman clutching her baby comes from the world of Auschwitz, but also of Bosnia or Burundi, of Vietnam, of the Congo, or any of the hundreds of atrocity-ridden wars waged against the weak and the poor. It is clear that 1945 did not mean the end of Fascism in Europe. Bond had earlier written a poem for the Hamburger Schauspielhaus to commemorate the fiftieth anniversary of the end of the war. It turned out to be a significant pointer towards the character of the Old Woman in the play:

The Face

I saw a woman sitting alone
And she was old old old
A heap of skin and bone
Her rags were knotted round her
But she shivered in the cold
She cried and as the tears fell on her face
They turned to stone

And in her face I saw the sufferings of her age
Years in the cells and labour camps
The months of questioning
Prisoners paraded to watch executions
Children lining up to die
The bowls of water-gruel – the crusts of bread
The dying stealing from the dead
To stay alive
The naked feet of marchers driven through the snow
In her grey hairs I saw the wisps of smoke from ashen rafters
She cried and as the tears fell on her face
They turned to stone

I said old woman do not weep
Today there is no cause to mourn
She said my son I weep because
I am not yet born

On 11 April 1995, Bond made this note to himself:

The play must be appropriate to the occasion: that is, an older writer addressing yps [young persons]. And so I should say what I consider to be important in that situation. The theme must be not only about adolescent problems. It must concern the choices which the world confronts them with. It's not a question of reminding them of mortality! – but of responsibility to transcend the classroom! – and its horizon of exams.

As well as positioning himself in relation to his audience, the note also sketches out what will become a significant theme: transcending the world of conventional schooling and the structure that contains the events of the play – exams, and their symbolic and actual function as ways of controlling young people. Even earlier, on 31 January, in his Bursary submission to the Arts Council, he states:

There must be a simple story – incident ... the story needs to be attached to some specific problem – but in order to use the problem as a larger illustration.

And in that submission he introduces one of the key underlying elements of what will become *At the Inland Sea*:

In a fairy-story, a witch is a 'problem'. But there are no real witches. So in a fairy-story a problem ('a witch') was used to explain life or some particular 'problems' in life. In a play about, say, drug-taking, drugs are a 'problem' in ways which witches aren't. We talk of 'cures' for drugs and other real 'problems'. A story about a witch is not a 'cure'. Art is not a 'cure'. *It provides patterns of reason and tension which organize our experience and give meaning to life.* [my italics]

There is a sense in which the fairy-story, or the folk-tale, underpins the play, though it is radically transformed. This is the literature with which generations of children have learned about the world, through metaphors of journeys, transformations, horrors, acts of heroism and treachery, living well and dying badly. Think of *Jack and the Beanstalk*. A boy and his mother need money to live. They send their cow to market (they depend on the cow, but they *are* desperate). The boy is waylaid by a man who takes the cow in exchange for magic beans. The magic beans grow into a giant beanstalk at the top of which is a castle, and a terrible, child-eating giant. The boy climbs the beanstalk and narrowly avoids being roasted alive in an oven. At the end of the story, he again avoids being killed by killing the giant. The mother and the boy live well because he has faced up to the worst that is possible and defeated it. Freudian psychologists, of whom the concentration-camp survivor Bruno Bettelheim is one, interpret the story in terms of the child's need to free himself from the mother (symbolized by the milk-giving cow Milky White) and establish his identity in the adult world by facing the terror and the challenge of adulthood (that giant might also be his father). This is interesting enough, but for Bond, the psychological pales into insignificance compared to the social reality that creates it. *At the Inland Sea* is far from being simply a conscious re-working of the fairy-tale genre, in the manner of Sondheim's *Into the Woods*. Indeed, in his notes of 22 May, he consciously distances himself from the genre:

> I don't want a folk/fairy-story which explains life by simplifying it – abstracting from it …

But the thinking about fairy-tales and their inadequacies ('the dreadful banality of the supernatural … I want to avoid any suggestion of fairy-tale. Young people will not take this seriously. I need to found the play in reality and solve its problems realistically') leads him on to a further stage of the pre-writing process. Now he extracts from the fairy-tale what is germane and useful – the idea of story, with its connotations of structure and a matrix of meaning – and leaves behind what is not – the supernatural and the moralistic. Thus, by the end of May, Bond is asking himself these potent questions:

> What story would you write on the side of a tank? … *What is the tale the mother told her little child as she huddled with it in the gas chamber?* … The tale of the mother in Hiroshima; she's dying in the burning street, can't take her child out – so sits and tells a tale as the fire burns its way towards them … 'What is the Real Story?' – this could almost be the title. [my italics]

The play is both breathtaking and demanding, as must any play be that takes its audience and main character from his bedroom in the present to the inside of an Auschwitz gas chamber as cyanide gas chokes its packed victims to death, and back to the present again. Often the language is dense and the action surprising, if judged in terms of ordinary television naturalism. It was one of the revelations of the tour to schools that such a long play (for young people's theatre), in a style far removed from its audiences' usual experience and about profoundly disturbing historical events, should nevertheless hold most of its audiences' attention. That is not to say that everything was 'clear' – on the contrary, the very richness of experience could be both confusing and stimulating. As one teacher told the only national paper to review the play:

> Because most of their experience of drama is via television and film, they are pretty much locked into naturalism as an approach. Once they'd got past that, they were impressed with the power of the play before anything was said about understanding it. Once

they'd realized that what they were watching was not a slice of life, they understood that there were connections there for them to draw. It doesn't preach at you, it leaves the audience to do its own work.

W. Stephen Gilbert, in the *Independent*, 29 November 1995

Like *Jack and the Beanstalk*, *At the Inland Sea* begins with a woman, her son, and problems of everyday survival. They need something to relieve them of their poverty, and their 'cow' is the boy's ability to get a job in a world where jobs are scarce and, such is the logic of the market economy, getting scarcer. The boy has only himself to sell at the labour market. His mother already does this, working on a super-market check-out.

What happens at the play's beginning seems bone-simple. A boy gets ready to go to school to sit exams. His mum bustles around, anxious for him, proud of him. On the surface, it is a scene of almost soap-opera banality. But there are undercurrents. Mum is anxious that he won't pass because he doesn't concentrate:

Always staring out the window. I think you'll end up a window cleaner.

She's aware of what's at stake in the harsh world outside:

I wish I was doing exams. Working for my boss – you need a degree in slavery. God knows I've done the studying.

Then, into this ultra-domestic, recognizable world, the extraordinary, the utterly unforeseen comes:

The **Boy** *starts to tremble slightly. He steadies the mug with both hands and wedges it against his chest. His head rises a little as if he looked at something beyond the room but his eyes focus on space just in front of him.*

The boy who stares out of windows – imagining – is no longer alone in his room. A woman has risen from the bed. She is in ragged clothes, and carries a baby wrapped in a bundle. She is the very image of atrocity and disaster, and her first words, half-sung, are 'The world's a stone. The world's a stone.'

In this extraordinary moment are all the built-in clues that tell the audience how to work with the whole play. We are in a world where the extraordinary invades the ordinary, where the past – or the geograph-ically distant present – can intrude upon the everyday. If this play were naturalistic, like the TV soaps it lightly invokes at the very beginning, the moment would be absurd. However, in theatre, actions can create their own logic; can, in effect, create the imaginative tools with which to 'read' the performance. What Bond does here is say, through this image of physical action, that it is possible for this kid in a room to be the cause of profound and apparently miraculous happenings. And because he is so 'ordinary', we can identify with him, sense something of the extraordinary in ourselves. We also have to deal, at some level of our minds, with what is causing this thing to happen. There are implied questions, whose answering stimulates the juices of imaginative understanding that are necessary for the whole play:

What is it about the boy that causes him to tremble, and then see?
Is he specially receptive? (Yes, his Mum's dropped hints about it.)
Is he unique in this? (No, we are seeing it too!)

Of course, there are precedents in the literature of childhood for visitations from people who have terrible tales to tell. We are in familiar and unfamiliar territory at the same time. Because there is no easy way now to predict what's going to happen next, we concentrate fully. The language is both clean and weighty. The images conjured in our minds – 'The world's a stone' – act like spice to the imagination, setting the juices flowing.

It is also characteristic of Bond's technique to choose very carefully what objects and actions the audience sees. The cup of tea that the Boy brings in is not naturalistic set-dressing, designed to give the illusion of the everyday. It has a specific dramatic use, like other, similar uses of the domestic mundane in, for instance, *Saved*, *Olly's Prison* or *Summer*. When, propelled by the horror of her situation and the Boy's receptivity, a woman gassed at Auschwitz enters his room more than fifty years later, the Boy's shock is first registered by his move to the chair where:

He sits huddled, clasping the cup.

Some moments later . . .

Slowly the **Boy**'s *arm straightens – he holds out the cup to the* **Woman**.

It is a gesture of simple, fundamental pity, an instinctive reaction, but it also shows an instinctive curiosity about the Woman. He needs to *know* what this thing is. As the Boy is held by the sight of the suffering Woman and her ragged baby, his hand tilts:

The tea starts to drip from the cup and then slowly spill.

(For at least one group of young people who saw the play, the most powerfully recollected image was that slowly tilting, spilling cup.) Already the Boy is moving into a different mode, a different 'world'. His Mother, bustling around him, notices the proffered cup, but not that the tea is spilt. A little later she sees the spilt tea and tries to take the cup away. In the process of pulling it away from the Boy who is no longer 'there', the cup gets broken. The mundane agent of mediation between the Boy and the ordinary world of schools and supermarkets he lives in – the cup – is broken. Later in the play, a man is described deliberately spilling crystals from a tin into a cement room full of people, and so there is a tension created between the two that asks a question – 'Is there a connection between the two? Can this Boy possibly become a man who gasses people – a mass murderer?' So the cup isn't just an abstract symbol, but it is part of a theatre language of meaning that the play creates for us to understand it. Nothing in the play is meaning-less, and the play creates its own keys to understanding.

Because the story is, in a sense, about the making of theatre itself – with the Boy's imagination channelling extraordinary phenomena into the stage of his bedroom – the conventions that govern how this happens are not fixed. That real Woman from the real and terrible past who turns up in a Boy's bedroom is not a simple figment of his imagination, but she is there because her need for survival, her need for justice is so overwhelming (and in this she stands for all the victims, all the dead and damaged of our age of power). Try and work out the logic behind this, as you would if this were some kind of science-fiction fantasy, and the explanation seems silly. Even more so when in Scene Four an Old Woman from some distant future appears to cast a mocking light on the obscenities of the twentieth century. However, once these events are enacted as theatre, as living, feeling metaphors, the logic becomes the story-telling logic of Theatre. Jack *can* make magic beans grow into a beanstalk.

The essential link between Theatre and Imagination, for Bond, is not simply that Theatre uses the audience's Imagination to function, but that Theatre itself *is* Imagination, made concrete and vivid in real time and space. The Boy's bedroom is *his* theatre. The Woman from Auschwitz comes out of his bed, the place of procreation and the place of dreams, both functions of creativity. It is the power of her suffering that forces her, against all the laws of space–time physics, all the tenets of 'common sense', into his room, yet her journey there is absolutely in accord with the laws of theatre. She is not a product of his imagination, but having arrived there, she challenges his imagination, even to the extent that he has to go with her into the gas chamber. He has to contemplate the horror of it, and consider how and why he should act in regard to it. The Woman's constant demand is for a story, because she understands that stories have special power. In so doing she instinctively acknowledges that art matters. The question that hangs over the play is 'What story, told to whom?'

The appearance of the Old Woman in Scene Four changes the conventional ground rules again. This time, the Boy's Mother can see her. It is as if he has infected his Mother with this power (this everyday, so *human* power – we are not in the realms of Superman or the Power Rangers here) in a way that makes sense as a theatre fact, if not as physical or even metaphysical logic.

The scene also re-uses the energy built up by the necessarily intense gas-chamber scenes before it. At first it feels like a relaxing scene, but the tension doesn't evaporate, it switches into another mode – a releasing contrast to horror. The preceding scene ended with the Zyklon-B crystals poured into the gas chamber by the man on the roof (a giant in boots), and the Boy taking the baby out of the chamber (or at least out of the scene, because no one can get out of a gas chamber, but the Boy *can* leave the *theatre* space). The scene ends with the people gasping out their dying pleas for a story that will save them.

In Scene Four, we're back in the Boy's bedroom, this time with the Mother on the bed, that place of creation and dreaming. She's exhausted and half-asleep. She hears a noise, but it isn't her son. An extraordinary vision enters. As the stage directions have it:

> A very **Old Woman** comes in. Her hair is beautiful and white and flows down to her knees. She wears an old, loose-fitting white smock and a comfortable old straw hat – half-way between a boater and a sunhat. The rim is a little dented and frayed and is decorated with an artificial flower. Her face looks like a linen mask.

The effect is mildly comic, and when the Boy comes in carrying the baby he took from the gas chamber, her gently smutty innuendo confirms the impression:

> (*little giggle*) You're in trouble. Your mother'll give it to you now!

Bond has also hinted that there's something of Raymond Briggs's dancing snowmen about her. Like them, she has a comfortable, generous presence, at home in the snow, light on her feet, with a straw hat and something of the galumphing child about her. As the scene builds, comedy becomes almost the content of the scene, as much as the mode in which it operates. We have to evaluate what laughter is – what it *means*. As the Boy, shocked, tells her what is happening/has happened in the gas chamber, the Old Woman starts to laugh. Not out of cruelty, certainly not out of indifference, but apparently out of sheer astonishment that such horrors could ever have been committed. She has her own store of atrocity stories, which she tells, and they reduce her to helpless laughter as well as forcing, at the very least, profoundly disturbing smiles and laughter from the audience!

When the Boy can stand no more of this, the Old Woman, so knowing, so sorted, lifts her smock. Beneath is all the evidence that her sense of the comic absurdity of human evil is not naïve or ignorant. She wears the history of the world underneath her white smock. It is 'a dress, filthy, bloody, torn, scorched, soot-marked, foul with corruption'. Images and stories of disaster and atrocity are caked upon it. It is a piece of pure theatre design, simple and rich, that conveys meaning rather than decorating the action. Now the Boy's Mother becomes a child herself, crouching beneath the smock to touch the scenes of devastation, to learn, at least for a moment, that her own sufferings and anxieties are shared. When at last the Old Woman makes to leave, she reveals who, or what, she is:

He thinks I'm old. I'm not yet born. One day I will be. One day I'll live on this earth.

She has already delivered this most damning of judgements:

All this, all this, there was no need. It didn't have to be. People blown in the wind. The storm. No need.

This is far from being a Utopian vision of the future. In spite of her assertion that 'When it's gone – all of it – I'll be born' the scene does not say that, in the future in some vague way, eventually all will be well, and we must bide with patience. The challenge that the Old Woman presents to the Boy and his Mother in that small bedroom is to take responsibility for, to take account of, the suffering of the past. Bond writes:

If we don't accept responsibility for the past I think we can't accept responsibility for the future ... I think the Old Woman's laughter at us is more disturbing than if she berated us and was angry with us. It 'cuts us down to size', it's not nice to seem ridiculous ... (bad) tragedy can be quite comfortable, whereas comedy disturbs us.

It is a moment of calm and knowledge, and it comes about because the Old Woman has come into the theatres of the Mother's, and the Boy's, minds. She leaves the room, sobered and serious. It is as if her laughter was at first uncontrolled, but now her reasoning has brought her back to earth. In the space of calm created by her presence, the Boy knows that, though he has to take responsibility for the past that includes the concentration camps, he cannot change history. This is *not* the world of *Back to the Future*. He knows that the baby died with his mother. In Scene Five, he is back once again in the gas chamber with the dying, and although horror pours back in, he has a chance at least of learning from it.

After the Boy's visit to the death chamber and his struggle to deal with the unimaginable horror of what he – and we – are nonetheless imagining, he is returned to his bedroom, his world, his everyday life. What he has experienced has been a rite of passage into adulthood, an entering into full humanity through it. But in the way of so many Bond play endings, there are no magical transformations. Certainly there is learning and possibility for him, and for his Mother too, but for her the picture is more ambiguous. Although they moved away from this position later, in the first run the company felt that the Mother's situation at the play's end was distinctly bleak. As director Geoff Gillham noted:

> It is extremely questionable whether he will be able to shift her. We felt that the mother was an example of someone whose imagination has been corrupted at every turn. Not that she hasn't gone through something but because she's conscious ... that's the potency of ideology and material circumstances. So we very much showed that she was a husk.

Preparing the Ground – the Company and the Workshop

A Theatre-in-Education company is a team of professional actor—teachers who work in schools and colleges. Big Brum doesn't follow the classic pattern of those companies that blossomed in the 1960s and 70s, who were mainly offshoots of regional repertory theatres. Instead it began as a stand-alone company set up specifically to work in TiE. Its programmes of work have visited junior schools and youth and community centres, but its main focus since its founding in 1982 (by new graduates Peter Wynne-Willson and Jan Page) has been on work for secondary school students. Although other TiE companies over the years have had similar work profiles, what marks Big Brum out so far is that it, at least, was still operational in 1995. The devastation visited on the institutional form of TiE, largely through Government education funding policies, has left a once vital movement shrunken and struggling. Big Brum has more than once come near to collapse and continues its work under constant threat from economic and political policies that oppose its work. It was in this context that the company approached a writer who they felt confident would share their artistic passions, their objectives, and their commitment to education.

When the process of negotiation about the commission began, the company had no special brief for the writer to deal with a particular subject or issue. Bond spent time with them, listening and questioning, during the last months of 1994. Out of this cautious and testing process came enough trust to persuade him to undertake the commission. As a writer, he has been wary about accepting commissions and productions from professional companies in Britain, where he feels the demands – of artistic practice and political understanding – his work places upon theatre artists are rarely understood and the results often distorted. As a result, he has instead maintained growing links with youth, community and arts education groups. One notable collaboration in 1979 was with students in Newcastle who first staged his play *The Worlds*. This play was revived later that year by The Activists, the young people's theatre company based at the Royal Court Theatre. As a writer nurtured by the Royal Court during the late Fifties and

Sixties, Bond clearly felt a particular responsibility to the group, and the set of essays and poems called *The Activists Papers* (published with *The Worlds*) mark a significant step forward in his thinking about theatre and society. In 1989, the two plays collectively titled *Jackets* were performed, first by students from Lancaster, and then by the Youth Theatre department of Leicester's Haymarket Theatre. Typically, Bond will rate a production of one of his plays by a youth group in Newcastle, or an amateur community theatre in Wales, more highly than one at the National Theatre or the RSC, and when he does venture into those big national institutions, the friction between writer and organization can be unproductively prickly. (Bond considers some of these problems in revealing and often uncompromisingly frank detail in his published letters, edited by Ian Stuart.)

It was Bond's idea to focus on an area of investigation – the Imagination – for the play, but it happened precisely to fit the company's concerns and thinking (as well as following current TiE practice in thinking beyond current issues to the deeper level of concepts that underlie human behaviour). Above all, the characteristic mode of Bond's work, which might be characterized as 'Theatre for Knowing', promised to fit closely with that of the company.

Roles and Reality

Because Big Brum is primarily a Theatre-in-Education company, *At the Inland Sea* was always going to be more than a play they performed in a school hall and then drove off to another venue to perform all over again. The TiE programme was devised and written for school students in their teens. The play was just one part – but a very significant part – of a whole day 'programme' offered to schools. Accompanying it was a participatory drama workshop, involving actors and students together, designed to be an equal partner to the performance, the one balancing and amplifying the other.

Active participation of the 'audience' itself in the world created by the drama was the characteristic technical innovation that Theatre-in-Education brought to theatre art. (That is, it offered something more than an active *imaginative* engagement by sitting and watching.) Sometimes participation is built into the dramatic action of the play itself. The individual 'audience' members will be asked to assume a particular role – not a character that they have to 'act' – that is appropriate to the play's world, and invited to share the action of the play with characters from it. By doing this they are able to join with the characters in unravelling the puzzles, and feeling the implications, of the play's story. It is not, properly done, an exposing experience because there is no 'acting' involved. There *is* pretence, as the individual student uses her imagination to put herself into a new situation. The role that the student adopts will usually be social, such as a cleaner, doctor, soldier, or reporter. She is not expected to be anyone else but herself, however, only to imagine *herself* as a cleaner, doctor, soldier, reporter or whatever. As the work progresses, imagination is used to work on the dramatic situation. Although the student is asked, at increasingly subtle levels, to think about 'How does my character feel in this situation?', there is never any question of acting the character's surface. No voices, funny walks or psychological tics are looked for – only decisions about what that character might feel and do in that situation. And the age, class, gender or race of the role-player are usually quite irrelevant to the task of representing the person dramatically. In the words of one Big Brum document (and this can stand for all serious TiE work):

> We believe that drama is a way of knowing: that through the
> safety of a fictional context we can begin to explore the most
> fundamental and taboo areas of human experience, and to begin
> to understand the world in which we live . . . we know that play is a
> serious activity for children, that education is a process, and that
> children are active seekers of knowledge . . . Working always
> within the safety of a fiction, Big Brum is able to explore those
> areas of human experience which do not lend themselves to easy
> answers.

Almost all worthwhile TiE workshops are intended for one class only, or smaller numbers. They can be held after the performance or before it. Post-play workshops – on balance perhaps the more common – will usually explore material from the play by using drama experiences. For example, a common, if basic, technique is to 'hot-seat' the characters (as played by the actors) from the play – that is, the audience are invited to talk to them about their actions and motivations in the play. Actor–teachers, as their twofold name suggests, need to be able to stay 'in character' during these improvised interrogations, but also aware of what the strategic, educational objective of the whole exercise is. Actor–teachers, in this respect, are particularly suited to performing Bond's texts, where playing an immediate situation has to be held in balance with a sense of what the total meaning and objective of the play is. Another, potentially more sophisticated, tool is the use of 'imaging', in which the students construct a three-dimensional symbolic representation of a moment, a feeling, or a concept, using themselves as the material of the 'sculpture'.

Pre-play workshops deal with similar material, and here the emphasis is likely to be on the concepts treated by the play that is to follow. This is not the same exercise as researching the background to a Shakespeare play before you go to see it. It is less an exercise in clarification or contextualization, more an exploration of the 'learning areas' that the play deals with. The workshop focuses the class's perceptions so that the experience of watching the play is deepened and the learning experience made more potent.

This was the style of work with which Bond was making direct contact when he accepted the Big Brum commission. Money, however, had to be found to pay for the commission and though the Arts Council paid for half of the writer's fee in the form of a Bursary, half had to come from company funds. Big Brum's core funding comes from West Midlands Arts (one of the Regional Arts Boards) and Birmingham Education Authority. In addition, a number of smaller arts and educational trusts contributed to the project, but it was still necessary for schools to pay for the company's visit. It was once common for local authorities to pay for all TiE work in their schools, but since the slash-and-burn policies of the 1980s against subsidy and local government, this practice is now mostly a dim memory. For the £140 that schools paid for the Big Brum programme, they received, on-site for a day, the skills of three talented and committed specialist actor–teachers, a designer–stage manager–sound manager, a package of teacher support material and, at one remove as it were, the services of an experienced director and an internationally admired playwright. Even in crude value-for-money terms, the package was transparently good value! However, this was still in a context where sound school buildings and unstressed school teachers are often barely affordable. Schools under pressure financially often cannot easily justify expenditure like this, and though the first tour was thankfully fully booked, some schools who wanted the programme were too pushed financially to consider taking it.

At the Inland Sea – **The Workshop(s)**

One of the standard practices in TiE work is to hold a Teachers' Workshop a week or so before the company begins the run. This allows teachers access to the programme in time to integrate what it has to offer into their own teaching plans. In the case of *At the Inland Sea*, the company didn't want to tell the schools too much about the play itself, as opposed to dealing with the content area – Imagination – that they and the writer wanted to emphasize. In part this was because they didn't want the play to be seen as 'about' Auschwitz, Fascism, European History, etc. (though all these content areas are fruitfully available because of the programme), with teachers feeling they needed to mug up on those subjects. Without actually misleading the teachers, a way was found to bridge the ground between the play's material and the overall learning area of Imagination. Gillham devised an exercise around the Bond 'Notes on the Imagination', which include the provocative statement that supermarkets are continuations of concentration camps.

I said, you may or may not disagree with that – we're not debating that at the moment – what I want you to do in your group is to take that as a premise and discuss how is a supermarket like a concentration camp. And they went for it! They thought of all kinds of things we hadn't. They were just buzzing about it when they came back to plenary. Barcodes – that's like stamping a number on you. They just opened and blossomed! The teachers were wonderfully trusting – they did trust us not to tell them much about the play.

The workshop that partnered *At the Inland Sea* took place before the performance, usually in the morning before lunch, with the play in the afternoon. It was developed during the main rehearsal period by the company led by Gillham. Though developed in too short a time by all the team's standards, the workshop clearly arose organically from the play, dealing with the central concept to which it gives living, sensuous shape – the human imagination. The workshop was, in effect, a work of art complementing the play, rather than a subservient preparation for it.

The initial tour of the whole play/workshop package took in a number of secondary schools in the Midlands region – from Birmingham, where the company is based, to nearby Smethwick, Coventry, West Bromwich, and further afield to Leicester and Northampton. Travelling in the company's vehicle, the three actor–teachers and designer–stage manager Michael Irving typically arrived two hours before the morning workshop began, unloaded, and put up the set, costumes, lighting and sound rig. All schools had received a booking sheet laying out the company's needs in terms of power supply, blackout and access to the space, but no TiE team can ever bet on not being interrupted by curious kids, dinner ladies who hadn't been told their hall was to be occupied when they needed it, or disgruntled staff who weren't going to see anything of the apparent treat for another class.

What follows is an evocation of the workshop as an experience. A word of caution here: each workshop was an event, unique and unrepeatable, like a performance but far more so. Each school is different, each class, each individual class member brings a different energy to the workshop, and the structure of the workshop itself evolves as the actor–teachers learn from the experience of doing it. Sometimes the Big Brum workshop 'worked' well, sometimes it was difficult. In the same way that a lesson can go well or badly, almost irrespective of its fundamental soundness, so the TiE workshop is variable in far less subtle ways than would be true of a performance.

I   What happens

In the following description, the names are those of the three actor–teachers in the Big Brum production, Bobby Colvill, Mandy Finney and Terina Talbot. The workshop's facilitator on the first run was Bobby Colvill, though here, as in most TiE work, there is no direct relationship between the facilitator role and any character played later in the play. The interpolated quotations in italics are from an observed workshop. They're not intended to represent what happened in all workshops, nor what was angled for by these actor–teachers, and certainly not what any other company should seek to *get*. They're offered here to give readers a basic sense of what one class offered within the hearing of one observer.

The three actor–teachers meet the class, who sit in a circle. Sometimes the class teacher will sit with them, sometimes they will want to keep a low profile – this decision is another factor in the overall dynamic of the work. Big Brum simply made a point of inviting the teachers, if they wished, to use the opportunity to observe their students. The actor–teachers sit in amongst the students. Bobby introduces the team, and after a few words about the company and the plan for the day, begins the workshop with some preliminary questions about the students, whether they've done drama before, what sort of thing they have done, and so on. The content is casual and friendly, but the form, a dialogue between students and facilitator, sets the pattern of the morning's work. Then he introduces the idea offered for exploration – the Imagination.

There is some open-ended questioning about how, when and why we use Imagination in everyday life: *English ... stories ... to entertain ... tell morals ... drama ... sometimes in science when you have to imagine atoms and molecules and things ...* The discussion moves on to consider stories encountered as children: *Red Riding Hood ... Cinderella ... Sleeping Beauty ...* Now Bobby sets up an exercise with the students in pairs. Each person tells his partner about stories they were told as a child, and where they were when they were told. The class are beginning to use their imaginations – as memory – recreating a place and time and feeling. These memories are shared in the whole group, and out of it come ideas about the violence of some of the nursery stories, such as *Red Riding Hood* and *Jack and the Beanstalk*. At the same time, they communicate their memories of childhood experiences (where they were for the stories) to the group.

The discussion moves on to stories adults tell and listen to: *Stephen King ... horror stories ... films about monsters ...* Bobby puts the question 'Are there really human monsters?' *Hitler ... child-killers ... but they don't look like monsters ...*

The discussion shifts into the difference between *fantasy* as escape from reality and *imagination* used to change reality.

II   Into role ...

(As the run progressed, Colvill moved into role much earlier on as one of the cleaners himself, though his facilitating function continued as before.)

Bobby now asks the class to take a space for themselves in the room, and to imagine that they are in an art gallery. They are not visitors, but cleaners. Gradually, using questioning, Bobby helps the class to build up a picture of the gallery, of the cleaners' relationship to it, and of their reactions to the works of art on display.

'Where does most dirt collect?'
'What's the floor like?'
'What do visitors think about the gallery?'
'What do kids like and what don't they like?'

The questions vary depending upon what is offered from the class. Now they are asked to imagine a particular painting that is in front of them. Whereas before the imaginative work emphasized the collective reactions of the cleaners, now they are creating individually. Bobby asks for individual reactions to the 'pictures' to be shared with the whole group:

'What does this picture make you feel about the world?'
'What does it mean to a kid on a council estate?'
'What are the people like in these pictures?'

They are asked to imagine the tool they use most as a cleaner, to hold it, weigh it in their hands, note what it looks like and feels like. Then they are asked to move to a place they clean every day, and to think about the person responsible for the dirt or rubbish on the floor.

'What do you feel about that person?'
'Look at your hands as you clear up the mess. What were your mum's hands like when you were a small child?'
'What did your mum want for you, when you were small? As you look at that picture on the wall, think about what you would want for the future.'

Again, a touch on individual shoulders elicits thoughts spoken about the pictures, and the cleaners' thoughts about their futures. It is noticeable that the 'picture' seen in a student's mind's eye prompts significant thoughts about the future:

A royal person in a portrait – I want something for my kids. Better than me.
Children playing – I want education I missed at school. Now I regret it.
A landscape – I want to get out of the city.

Abstract, mess – My life's a mess. Trouble with bills.
A beautiful palace – It looks out of this world and I want to go there.

The students here are, in imagination, 'cleaners', but they are clearly letting their own concerns and feelings bleed through that membrane that separates themselves from their roles.

III   Digging deeper

Now there is a new input from Bobby. The cleaners have a tea-break and sit around talking to their friends about something disruptive and upsetting that's happened in their lives. Each 'cleaner' decides on what the thing should be, and shares it. Their image of their particular 'cleaner' is becoming richer, but the enrichment comes from their own imaginative experience.

For a few moments, they are asked to drop out of role and to answer some questions about 'their' cleaners' lives. There is no 'side' to these questions, and there is still no question of looking for 'character' to perform, just a deepening of their knowledge of the people they have invented and now stand for. Bobby, as facilitator, is working to a structure but he has to be flexible enough, and listen closely enough, to take on board what the students offer. What they say is not fed by the actor–teacher, whose facilitating job is to enable them to articulate their feelings and ideas in a useful way so that the work can be moved on.

IV   The artist at work

The session shifts into another gear. Mandy is in role as an artist and the students are asked to come out of their roles and observe the sequence. She uses materials that she has already brought to the gallery – plastic milk crates, a grey and brown-streaked sheet folded into a bundle that suggests there might be a baby inside, a piece of mottled grey board about the area of a grave, a sack of dry earth, a plank of wood, a picture of flowers, a grey concrete block. (The 'artist' is actually re-creating an exercise that formed part of the workshop development process during rehearsal – hence the unpretentiousness of the materials!) The artist combines the objects into an assemblage, or sculpture. Again, the end product varied, depending on how the 'artist' actor–teacher decided to make her assemblage. This made it easier for the company to come afresh to the students' reactions because they weren't even sure what was being offered to them until it happened! On one day, this is what the artist assembled: the grey board 'grave' lines up with a kind of see-saw structure made from the plank and the milk crates. Lying in line with the see-saw, about a metre away, is the bundle. The artist pours the earth onto the board, and spreads it around, then writes with her finger in the dirt 'Dust to dust'. (The whole is suggestive rather than representational and the words necessarily used here may already invest the work with more predigested 'meaning' than was apparent to the students.) When the artist has finished work, she leaves a notice, inviting the public to change the sculpture if they want to, but to 'leave it as you would wish others to meet it'. Though not reducible to a single meaning, the assemblage does suggest the bones of a narrative, with its two archetypal images of birth and death. In so doing, it offers the students ideas of life and art, and what might be the relationship between them.

V   Interpreting the art

Bobby now sets up a new scenario. The cleaners arrive at work the next morning. As cleaners, the students are asked to pick up their cleaning tools, which means they have to pass the newly assembled sculpture. By this stage of the session, they are perfectly well able to move in and out of role without further prompting, and as they approach the artwork, they begin to react as cleaners. Their feelings and perceptions come pouring out – some contradictory, some perceptive, some clichéd. What is significant is that they are listening to one another, so that ideas and feelings are shared, ostensibly between the cleaners but actually between the students. The role acts to protect them from the negative aspects of peer pressure.

> *Bit sick . . . Babies and graves . . . Babies and graves is life, isn't it? . . . It's real . . . Too morbid to think about . . . Nothing to do with us . . . Yes it has – it's in my way . . . If we carry on these jobs, we'll end up like that . . . We're not babies, are we? . . . I'd rather have a nice picture of a sunset . . . Someone's getting paid to make that . . . It says you can touch it . . . That means visitors, not us . . . We're just cleaners . . . It doesn't say 'Cleaners can't touch' . . . We have to look at it whether we like it or not . . . Respect it, it's a picture, you respect the others . . . It's just a pile of dirt.*

(There was a frequent desire noted by the team for students to want the baby bundle moved away from the grave, as if to find space for it away from the icon of death.)

Back out of role, there's a discussion led by Bobby about what the cleaners' reactions mean. There's a mix of comments about their cleaner's feelings, as well as direct responses to the artwork from themselves. The area between role and individual student is negotiated freely, allowing students to operate at whatever level they find most comfortable. Their interpretations of the artwork are usually thoughtful and engaged, in particular picking up on the possible implied meaning of a birth-to-death journey implicit in the artwork. The level at which the class operates is also, of course, a function of the 'tone' of its leading. The skilled drama teacher or actor-teacher will establish both a friendliness of personal contact with a manner that says: 'This work is significant and serious, and we will honour the students' work as significant and serious.'

Now they are asked to go back into role and the cleaners' working day has moved on to a tea-break. But the presence of the artwork continues to haunt them, and they continue to discuss its meaning for them and their lives:

> *It's got to be moved . . . It's disgusting . . . Leave it, respect it, even if you don't like it . . . People who want to move it just can't face up to their own lives . . . Babies are dying on TV – this is real life . . . You don't always want to see babies dying . . . Everybody has a life before they die . . . Except in war . . . What disturbs you the most? The baby? Let's remove it. Who wants to move the baby?*

In the school where this exchange took place, a 'cleaner' picked up the baby bundle and threw it across the dirt 'grave'. This was an uncanny pre-echo of a moment in the play, which originally suggested the image of the bundle of rags that might hold an infant.

> *What's it supposed to mean now? This sculpture – there must be something in it, the way it's getting to everybody . . . Someone's just destroyed someone's imagination . . . It's a mess now . . .*

Bobby drops some questions into their exchanges . . .
'What's in your lives that this sculpture has?'

> *Fear of death . . . Got nothing . . . Hard times . . . It reminds me of death . . . I don't want to see it . . . Everything in life gets broken . . .*

'What's going to happen next?'

> *Don't tell . . . Stick together . . . Put it back together . . . Get back to work and ignore it . . .*

'While you get on with work, think about your life, what's happening to you.'

VI   Intervention

Another actor–teacher (Terina) enters in role as a security officer in the gallery. She's noticed that the sculpture has been tampered with and asks the cleaners what they know about it. Initially their answers are defensive and noncommittal, but someone is brave enough to point out that people are *invited* to change it, and she points out the notice. There's an altercation between the cleaners, defending themselves, and the security officer, who insists that their feelings are neither here nor there, they're paid to clean the place, and the notice certainly doesn't refer to them! After the security guard has gone, the cleaners talk again about what has happened, and about the sculpture and its meanings. Some of them modify it again.

VII   Resolution and New Beginning

The students retain their roles as cleaners, but there is no 'action'. They stand in a space and Bobby moves amongst them, touching a shoulder to allow each one to voice his or her thoughts about what's happened that morning at the gallery.

> *There's life after death . . . We need money to help our children . . . Our hopes are in our children's lives . . . Perhaps it wasn't about children dying in war, but about children without a future . . . I can't change my life, that's why I believe in an afterlife . . . That's fantasy! Why not use your imagination to change your life now? . . . If you're a cleaner, unless you win the lottery, you're always the same . . . Death will come to the rich too.*

Finally, Bobby winds the session up with some questions to the class out of role:

'Would the artist have wanted all this to have happened?'
'What was the artist doing with their imagination?'
The morning drama workshop is closed.

It was a clear decision on the part of director and company that the workshop shouldn't deal directly with the specific situation or surface events of the afternoon's play. There is no reference here to concentration camps and gas chambers, nor to war and the atrocities that accompany it (which are the imagistic vehicle for a lot of the ideas of the play). The subjects for thinking (and feeling) about are art and the imagination, and how they might relate to the whole pattern of a life. Mandy Finney writes of the relationship between the workshop and the play:

> We found that not only did the workshop prepare them to watch the play, but the young people were continually touching on several images from the play, without having yet seen it . . . On numerous occasions, they virtually spoke lines from the play. It occurred to me that, in this, they were developing *our* understandings. They were teaching *us* about the play.

Focusing on Imagination keys the students into the play's main content, and also creates a way of looking at the play that answers the question 'What was the artist in the workshop (and also Edward Bond) doing with their imagination?' In the words of one 'cleaner', '*To provoke people's thoughts about how they live . . . so they can change.*'

At the pre-run meeting with teachers, it was suggested that in the first lesson after the visit they should not try to over-explain or intellectualize the experience of the play, nor encourage students to do so, but offer them a structure that would allow them to record their responses, partly to the play itself and partly to their own reactions to it. The company used the biblical image of Saint Veronica's Cloth – on his way to crucifixion a woman handed Christ a cloth to wipe his brow and it retained a perfect image of his face thereafter – as a metaphor for this process. The company wanted to encourage teachers and students to work artistically, rather than cerebrally, at least at first. It was suggested that teachers note the positions and image of the installation in the art gallery and use that image as the starting point for work, asking the class what changes they would make to it, or how might the boy, or his mother, the woman, the cleaners, change the installation.

Assessing the effect of Theatre-in-Education is fraught with difficulty because once the utilitarian culture of attainment targets and key stages are employed to judge Art, many cans of worms are opened. Straddling the artificially separate worlds of Art and Education, this theatre form challenges conventional National Curriculum-style assessment. Nevertheless everyone involved in this work craves intelligent feedback and constructive criticism. Comments like these from teachers were fairly typical:

> ... The workshop gently prepared them to watch the play ... shone lights on things ... helped me as teacher, and them, to understand what they'd experienced ...

> ... enjoyed watching my groups of students in the workshop ... skilled in creating dramatic tension which really brought the session to life ... session not threatening in any way ...

> ... play extremely challenging for my groups (and for me) and many of them came to the next lesson saying 'I didn't understand any of that'. After evaluation, it appeared we'd all grasped more than we thought from the performance ...

> ... liked the fact it wasn't naturalistic ... form useful as well as content ... things in it students could make use of ...

Perhaps most memorable, though not directly part of the educational purposes, was this poignant comment from a teacher:

> It was a pleasant experience for them that so much time was being concentrated on seventeen of them, and that Edward Bond had bothered to write for young people. This scared them, but also touched them and made them feel empowered.

*

The boy was very upset by the things the woman was asking. He found it hard to think of the story the woman wanted, or how a story could be of any use to her, if she was going to be killed by the man in boots. The boy's mother came in, and she could see that he was very upset, but the woman with her baby were invisible to her.

The next day the boy seemed to be ill, and his mother made him stay in bed. The woman with the baby was still there in the room, still begging him to help her. After a few days, the boy seemed to get better, and his mother came in to tell him that people had heard all about his hard work. She was so pleased and happy that now he would live well in the big world that she danced around and around his room, mad with happiness.

But the boy had once again seen the terrified woman and he could not celebrate with his mother, knowing that the woman and the child were going to die. This made his mother angry and she left his room . . .

*

Acting and Action

The major challenge for any company performing this, as any Bond play, is to find a way of acting it. These are less questions of sticking on a style that 'works', more of starting a radical reappraisal of what acting ought to be. This new thinking and practice has been an important part of Bond's work in recent years and is reflected in the amount of work he has done as a director of his own plays, and a leader of acting workshops all over the world. Indeed, it has moved forward hand-in-hand with his writing as the crises of global society call up from him not only a group of plays that address that overwhelming challenge, but also a means of acting them that will both reflect and generate the possibility of change. In particular, Bond the socialist dramatist believes that the conventional forms of socialist drama, in particular the work of Brecht and his many descendants, has now to be radically re-evaluated. He offers a move away from conventional socialist drama that, however powerfully, acts as a *transmitter* of socialist ideas. As one of the Big Brum actor–teachers, Mandy Finney, writes:

> I have watched many dramas on TV, and some theatre, which really tackle social issues and deal with pertinent questions of our time . . . And I have come away satisfied that they have confirmed my view of the world and how things are. But satisfaction and confirmation are not enough – they fall short of what is required. To have one's imagination made critical implies future action. It implies decisions about how we will live, in relation to what we've seen and heard. As Edward says later in the paper [Rough Notes on Theatre]: 'There is not an alternative insight or understanding. It is an out-sight which requires action.'

This work is ongoing, and practical, so it is not glibly transferrable into a method, though the starting points are becoming clear (and it may also become clear in these notes how closely these mirror many of the aims and practice of Theatre-in-Education). Perhaps the defining strategies of these emerging ideas about acting are these:

1. Engaging the audience's *critical* imagination to show the actions of characters as intelligible primarily as the results of social

interaction (whether between individuals, groups of people, or people and states).

2. Making individual incidents and images in the play resonate with meanings throughout the whole structure of the play.
3. Creating meaning out of every gesture, and every visual image (including props, costume, set), and directing those meanings to illuminate the whole structure of the play.
4. Allowing the use of imagination to be the primary activity for both actor and audience, rather than reason (as in Brecht) or feeling (as in Stanislavski).
5. Giving the audience a function in the theatre as active as that of the actors.

The main tool that Bond brings to bear on his own work with actors he calls a Theatre Event (TE). It's as much an approach as a technical device. In his own words:

> The strategy of TEs is: we select incidents in the story and open these incidents out in such a way that they can't be captured by the story but must be examined for themselves in relation to the story: then 'reality' may impose its interpretation on the story. *Of course I write in such a way not merely to make this possible – but to demand it.* [my italics]

Another way of understanding the Theatre Event idea is as a shift of emphasis from the *whole* play as a seamless event to a focus instead on key moments in each scene that are mined intensively for their meaning. In so doing, they resonate those meanings out through the whole body of the play.

During the rehearsal of *At the Inland Sea*, Bond both worked with the actors and kept up a steady stream of faxes and letters to them from his Cambridgeshire home. These were always welcomed as useful and challenging by the company, even when they made the work temporarily harder! During this process, though there were challenges, disagreements, and difficulties *en route*, the writer did not need to ask actors and director fundamentally to rethink their acting because the TiE mode already moves along the road towards his goal – acting that shows meaning and significance rather than simply behaviour. Not that this basis of common interest and trust made the problems automatically solvable without hard work. These actors, for all their willingness to learn and adapt, for all their experience of Drama Mode teaching and Theatre-in-Education performance, had all trained in conventional drama-school Stanislavskian techniques. And although Bond worked with the actors and director on one or two occasions, he did not – *could* not – offer them quick and easy solutions. As one of those actors, Mandy Finney, later wrote:

As we worked on the text with Edward, he continually placed
questions to the actors, such as, 'Why does she say that?' 'Why
does he use that word?' 'Why doesn't she look at him?' 'That's an
odd thing to say, isn't it?' He wasn't, as I think we had secretly
hoped, the fountain of knowledge and meaning. Even though he
wrote the words, he was genuinely exploring it with us . . . he
couldn't tell us how to do it. The 'how' of it was our problem.
Here, 'problem' is being understood as a positive thing. The
solving of problems contains learning and development. What
Edward did assert was, 'Don't play the character. Play the play.'

The approach to rehearsal implied in this is crystallized in the term
'use'. Bond wants his plays to be 'used' as tools for understanding.
This is clear enough for an audience, but the implication is that the
approach be carried into the rehearsal room from the beginning. Here
the director should, in Bond's words, 'make the problem multifaceted,
volatile, the opposite of concrete'. For this, he needs the actors' imaginations:

> The actors must find and act their own relationship to the text and
> no one else can do this for them. The point of rehearsals is to find
> the actor's wisdom and knowledge . . . he or she 'imitates' the
> character, but the imagination is the actor's reality, his or her hold
> on life – and the play will try to use this. So a text opens
> opportunities for use – it does not dictate performance.

Though much of the work was extremely detailed and complex,
especially in the close attention paid to language, imagery and structure, there was still sounding beneath it a note of fundamental story-
telling simplicity. As Bond wrote to the company after one session,

> If we can tell this story clearly and graphically to young people,
> we'll have done something valuable – a white sail will have risen
> out of the sea.

In rehearsal, the company worked with the writer on one speech,
'The Woman's Story: Waiting' from Scene Two, and later he wrote
out for them a detailed, line-by-line analysis of every sentence in it.
What's clear from that document is that not one image is arbitrary or
careless. Each image, whether crematorium-smoke stinging eyes, or
the gas chamber's hinges as huge iron fists, or the grass that is the last
the woman will ever tread on, is carefully chosen and precisely linked
to its neighbours, and to other, transformed versions throughout the
play:

> . . . to oblige the audience's minds to work, to be involved and not
> to turn away or not to even merely observe. The text uses basic
> classical imagery – all flesh is grass, dust to dust, ash to ashes, the

sky, soldiers, and mothers with children etc. It relates these to contemporary imagery: soldiers, gas, concrete. It contrasts time with 'eternity' – the train-schedules of destruction with the time of sky, birds, grass. It suggests that meaning must be seen in the change of things.

Working with a playwright who presents interpreters with complex problems and has strong ideas about solving them can be a difficult business, particularly for the director. A sense of the give and take involved in this relationship is given by the difference of emphasis over the situation the Mother finds herself in at the end of the play. Bond wanted more of a sense that she had learnt from the Boy and commented that the production didn't bring that out. Gillham and the company had felt that she was, in his phrase, 'a husk'. Bond's reaction was to concede that this too might be right, saying that he might be resisting his own play. At that moment the company individually all thought that he was right, at least, in this! However by the time of work on the second run of the play, the company had began to concur with Bond's original view of the Mother's situation. These changes and revaluations clearly indicate a fundamental trust and generosity in the process, but also illustrate the truth that characters can exert unexpected demands on both writers and performers, much as the Woman does on the Boy.

The work that all three actors had to do was clearly going to be taxing emotionally. Their characters had all to deal with the depths of human experience, and yet they had to make it available to young audiences in a way that was intense but *not* overwhelming. The framing device of the gassed woman visiting a 1990s kid already gives the terrible, banal detail of the gas chamber procedures a kind of distance without in any way diminishing its impact. The performer nevertheless has to find a means to work within the frame:

> I just knew that this play contained places that I did not want to go into . . . To work on this play felt like having to stare nothingness in the face. What I realized was, that if I was to take an audience there, and enable them to map it, I had to do the same.

Bond's note to the actors was, at all costs, to avoid pathos. The problem for the actor playing the Woman is what exactly she *should* play. For Mandy Finney, playing the Woman, the answer started to become clear in this note from Bond:

> As actors you do not need to express emotion, but to understand why your character is expressing emotion – this understanding will lead to the appropriate expression of the emotion. The emotion will not be able to become an end in itself.

For Finney, this was:

> ... an example of understanding and being conscious of how the text is written – the character, the Woman, describes her situation and what she is doing in the face of it, but she never tells us how she feels. So it wasn't requiring me to play how terrible it is. As Edward pointed out, we can take it as read that the gas chamber is terrible. What we need is to see it, know it, understand it. So the important thing is to create the pictures for the audience, letting the language speak for itself.

The Mother (of the contemporary Boy) also presents fascinating acting challenges. As Gillham suggests, the character rolls out a line of clichés in her opening speeches:

> ... but clichés are a holding form of ideology quite often. So in that section she can say: well they only come in to get a warm and welcome smile off me. Its like she's arguing with the boss but on the *terms* of the boss. In order to justify her irritation at home. So she knows it and doesn't know it at the same time. She knows it's an unacceptable system but she speaks for it all the time. Even though everything about her is in opposition to it.

The difficulty here is to play the contradictions and inconsistencies in the character – to play the twists and turns of thought for themselves, rather than to look for consistency of character, as a conventionally psychological acting approach might dictate.

For the director, Geoff Gillham, there was the additional objective of showing that these unnamed people are not abstract ciphers, for all that they are powerfully emblematic – mother, son, mother and baby, wise old woman. In rehearsal, he and the company worked to find an individuality, in particular a clear location in social class, that was placed at the service of each scene's situation, rather than being derived naturalistically from it. It is no coincidence that this process of gradually deepening the individuality of characters, without ever losing the primary focus of showing them in their social relationships to one another and to the world, closely mirrors the journey taken by the 'cleaners' students in the workshop.

Above all, for Gillham and the actors, the primary task was not to teach the classes of young people lessons in feeling. In this respect, although they obviously share core subject-matter, *At the Inland Sea* differs from a work like *Schindler's List*, whose main objective is to generate strong feeling for, and on behalf of, the victims of the Holocaust. In the Big Brum programme, on the other hand, the objective was always the *understanding* of a process, but understanding achieved sensuously, viscerally. The company consciously worked to Bond's own note that the play should *not* teach a philosophical–political truth, enforced through naturalism:

> The text does not say that Auschwitz, the Holocaust, brutality, waste are horrible, inhuman, cruel ... If it did, it would be doing the work of the audience. The audience must condemn Auschwitz – not be told it is being, or has been, condemned.

And the means for doing that in the theatre is yet again the Imagination:

> ... Instruction is destructive if imagination is not autonomous. You can be instructed in bricklaying. Who will teach you whether to build a hospital or a gas chamber? The imagination. We act humanly when our imagination recognizes the imagination in others, but only an autonomous imagination can do this because only it can recognize the human in itself. In a just society, we would map our imaginations onto the real world, and then our actions and even our economy and institutions would replicate our humanness.

> from Bond's 'Notes on the Imagination', published with his play *Coffee*

Edward Bond's Theatre of Human Responsibility

In a career that encompasses a productive span of nearly thirty-four years, Bond has produced a body of work that becomes in its way ever more experimental, testing the boundaries of what theatre can do in every individual aspect of craft – acting, writing, directing, designing. His work as a whole follows the pattern of someone like the composer Michael Tippett, resolutely creative into his nineties. Critics of his work sometimes describe it as cold and bleak, perhaps because the fierce objectivity of his vision doesn't sit easily with our conventional ideas about creative writing. The cliché that you must 'write what you know' combines with the Romantic artistic philosophy of self-revelation and self-expression to place great weight on the autobiographical in literature. Bond is clearly a writer who tends to filter his own biography and experience through that of imagined characters miles and years away from his own personal life. Nevertheless, there are constant echoes in his work of his own life experience. The soldiers who routinely kill and die throughout his plays bear the mundane imprint of his National Service in the 1950s, the characters from the Fens of East Anglia echo his own family's roots in that open, man-made, cloud-capped landscape. It is completely consistent with Bond's whole approach to writing that these autobiographical elements should be entirely at the service of the play and its function. It is, paradoxically, autobiographical writing that absolutely refuses to draw attention to the writer.

In the year of writing *At the Inland Sea* Bond turned sixty. The actual moment of the shift from fifty-nine to sixty occurred while he and his wife Elisabeth were watching an all-night performance of *The War Plays*, his formidable trilogy from 1985, at the Avignon festival in France. The production was hailed as a masterpiece by French critics, and the occasion must have resonated powerfully, given the painful frictions and general dissatisfaction that had surrounded the production of the same plays at the Royal Shakespeare Company ten years before. What is most striking about Bond's output, viewed from *At the Inland Sea*, is not just the vast creative and imaginative scope of his output, but its essential consistency. Of course, any one writer's work will bear all kinds of hallmarks of their preoccupations, experience, and technique, but in Bond's case there were powerful conjunctions of forces at work early on that continue to fuel his work today. Overwhelmingly, what characterizes that power is what he expressed in a 1972 interview:

> I suppose one starts scribbling, jotting, in order to solve a puzzle, *to find out exactly what it's like*. [my italics]

It is this powerful need to analyse, to understand, *to know*, that renders all his work political in the most profound sense, and ties it together with the twin threads at the heart of *At the Inland Sea* – education and imagination. As with other, mainly working-class writers of his generation, the education system had failed to recognize Bond's qualities or talents. War played its part in disrupting what formal education he did receive, in particular because he was evacuated from North London to Cornwall during the blitz. It was here – in a strange, cold house, looked after by a childless family that resented his sister and himself, miles from the bombing he assumed must be slaughtering his family – that the children comforted one another by telling stories, demonstrating the human need to articulate meaning in a hostile world that informs the play in this book. Almost every interview Bond has given at the various stages of his career resonates with the same ground bass of testing, interrogating, probing the world, solving problems – 'to find out what it's like'.

The lack of a decent formal education he has often reckoned as a liberation, requiring him ever after to educate himself. The consequence of this self-education was and is a vision of the world that has the urgency of questioning and the freshness of perception of a child. It's a reflection of how we abuse youth and childhood that we have to remind ourselves that a child's perception doesn't rule out sophistication, or profundity of understanding, or depth of feeling. One of the biggest mistakes our contemporary culture makes is to reject what is instinctively known about childhood – that it is central to human experience

– and to replace it with visions that are both sentimentalized and *faux-naïf* (geared to the demands of the market economy), and demonized and feared (controllable by corporate states threatened by the power of childhood and adolescence – what Bond calls 'radical innocence').

Bond's work is shot through with the idea and image of the young and their search for meaning, and a meaningful life, in a political culture where those things are the privileges of a lucky minority. It's there in his very first produced play, *The Pope's Wedding*. Set in an Essex village at the end of the Fifties, its central characters are a young lad called Scopey and an ancient recluse who lives in a wretched old hut. Scopey is just one of the local kids with no prospects other than to labour for the local landowner, hang out with the local boys, make a narrow marriage. One afternoon he achieves a moment of pure glory when he plays the game of his life for the village cricket team that defeats the local landowner's men. Thereafter, though his life returns to dull unfulfilment, he now can't help but demand more. The world he lives in can't recognize his right to a real life and he turns more and more to visiting an old recluse, Alen, who lives in a rough old hut on the edge of a field. It's as if in caring for him, assuming the stereotypical female role that he usurps from his wife, Scopey both rejects the narrow community of maleness and bravado, and also begins to feel that Alen has some secret, some strange knowledge that will give him the answers he needs. Alen, as it happens, has no answers, but Scopey *needs* them so much he murders the old man in despairing need to become him, to get inside him, to put on his filthy greatcoat and stare blankly out at the world in a mad attempt to see what Alen sees. When in a later play, *The Sea*, a young man seeks answers from an old recluse, he is told 'Don't trust the wise fool too much. What he knows matters and you die without it. But he never knows enough.'

Scopey is there in the Boy in *At the Inland Sea*. The Boy knows more about the world than Scopey, and he has taken the bait that passing exams will lend his life meaning. But passing them doesn't bring meaning, any more than winning a cricket match solves Scopey's problems. It is History, rising up from his bed, demanding to be recognized, that offers some possibility of it to the Boy. In this perspective we can see that, though the vision is more mature and the techniques more sophisticated, Bond's preoccupations, from his earliest to his most recent plays, have stayed in essence the same. 'Solving the puzzle, finding out what it's like' results in a literal dead-end for Scopey. For the Boy in this play, the struggle is no less hard, the experience no less painful, but the outcome now is potentially fruitful. The young people in Bond's play need to solve the puzzle, to find out what it's like, and as Bond himself engages with the problems of the contemporary world – not just as an artist but as a radical social critic – so for his young characters the possibilities of confronting the immense problems of the new millennium become clearer.

Bond retains a childlike vision because it is the child who demands more of the world and questions more of it than do most adults. (In his phrase, the child *radically interrogates* his surroundings.) Our problems as a society are that we fail to recognize that this interrogation, this testing of what the world is, can turn sour and impotent when the wrong answers are given, or when fantasized solutions – commercial, consumerist, nationalist, individualistic (pretty much the staple of conventional education) – are offered. The despair that turns the child-turning-adult to drug and alcohol abuse, suicide and violence is endemic and likely to increase unless our vision is lifted from the ground a few feet in front and focused on and over the horizon. It is this vision that Bond brings to his social analysis of the future of the world. The scope of that analysis might seem arrogant and over-ambitious were it not that the world shrinks ever-faster as information technology explodes and global markets establish themselves independently of nation-states and cultures: the problems a kid in London faces may be felt less sharply than his counterpart in an Iraqi village, but increasingly they stem from the same social and economic forces, over which neither has much control.

*

The woman with the baby needed the boy's help, his story, so badly that she led him by the hand, out of his room, out of his house, his street, his town, and back to her own time. She showed him the cave, and the people outside it, waiting to be killed. Then they were all pushed inside the dark cave. After a few moments, the man in boots started to stamp and dance above them, his stamping sounding like thunder. The people inside the cave were terrified, and the man in boots started pouring his magic crystals onto their heads to make them die. The boy wanted so much to help the woman that he took a baby he thought was the woman's, and he got back – he hardly knew how – to his own room again.

*

Theatre-in-Education – Movement Through Crisis

In his pioneering survey of the first fifteen or so years of the Theatre-in-Education form, *Learning Through Theatre* (published in 1980), editor Tony Jackson felt able to state that:

> Compared to the position at the beginning of the decade (the Seventies), the present situation looks decidedly encouraging. By and large some form of TiE even if on an infrequent basis is available in most of the major centres of population and in many of the rural areas as well. There has been, since the early 1970s, not only expansion but diversification.

Writing this barely one year into the New Right counter-revolution that sought to reverse the whole philosophical and ideological base upon which the best of state education, and its partner, Theatre-in-Education, was based, it was perhaps the last moment at which it was possible to be cheerful about the institutional future of the form in this country. Though Jackson himself goes on to foresee problems with both forthcoming cuts in state spending, and conservatism in the educational establishment, David Pammenter, a significant figure in the field and director of the Belgrade TiE team for some years, is presciently clear that 'given the priority of recent governments and the climate of cut-back created by the current one (1980), the future of TiE is bleaker than it has ever been'.

Anyone wanting a thoroughgoing survey of the founding impetus that launched the TiE form should read the essays in that book. In the mid-Nineties, mired in mean-spirited policies designed to reverse the post-war movement towards a progressive and egalitarian education system, it's clear that, in its short life, British TiE has evolved enormously in sophistication and a theoretical understanding of its own practices, precisely as it has been pushed further and further into a corner, with fewer and fewer full-time teams operating.

In the phase of TiE development marked, approximately, by Jackson's book (that is, roughly from the initial experiments in defining what the form actually was, to a period somewhere about the mid-Eighties), there was a broad consensus that the content of TiE programmes was derived from each team's desire, confirmed by their contacts with teachers, to explore significant issues that were of use and significance in the school. (The personnel of these early companies were often themselves products of the new post-war educational world, working-class and lower-middle-class people from the new comprehensives, and as such had ideas and passions about the state of the world and what to do about it.)

Typical of this work would be the many TiE programmes that concerned themselves with racism and/or sexism. Companies would often respond to initiatives from schools or funding bodies (in London, for instance, the Inner London Education Authority), to produce a variety of work that dealt with these urgent and immediate topics. During the 1970s, a resurgence of Far Right activity in the inner cities where many companies operated seemed to demand urgent and practical responses from the TiE teams. Companies such as Theatre Centre in London produced material using the whole panoply of TiE techniques – role-play, scripted theatre, drama workshops – and in Theatre Centre's case created a women's company, and an energetically multiracial approach to recruitment. Most companies, from a combination of wishing to take joint responsibility and *collective* control over their material, and a mistrust of the prevailing approaches of most conventional playwrights, devised (i.e. collectively authored) their own work.

Issue-based work such as this would often generate a need to understand the deeper concepts that lie beneath the issues. By the mid-Eighties, some companies, exemplified by the North London-based Cockpit TiE team of the period, moved to explore concepts felt to be significant to young people's learning, and to build drama experiences around these, a reversal of the earlier order of working. This was in part perhaps a political response to the artillery bombardment laid down by the Thatcher government against all liberal or socialist values and practice. The emphasis shifted from specific problems (issues) caused by that bombardment to trying to find the interconnectedness of the events that were happening and link them to a larger perspective about how reality – particularly political reality – works. This shift of focus came together with a parallel renewed interest in the work of Drama-in-Education practitioners, who, as a profession, were based in the schools and educational institutions, as opposed to theatres. The work of the Drama Teacher with students, though the 'issue' of, say, sexism may be a motivating starting-point, will more probably build her work from the underlying abstract idea of gender (of which the issue of gender stereotyping – sexism – is a part). In Drama work of this kind, the principle is to begin with particular human experience (usually that offered in class by the students themselves), work to find the universal in that, and return to the particular again, but at a higher point of understanding. One pioneer figure from the Drama-in-Education world, Dorothy Heathcote, has helpfully summarized three modes of education:

TRANSMISSION TEACHING, in which the teacher transmits information to the students possibly using other media to help, books, videos, computers, etc. How well this has been absorbed by the student is then assessed and tested in exams.

ENQUIRY SYSTEMS, in which the teacher seeks to understand and respond to how the child views the idea or subject under scrutiny.

DRAMA MODE, a synthesis of the other two. This is summed up by Heathcote like this: 'the teacher contributes and participates, the children co-operate (with each other and) with the participating teacher as well as they can, and they all end up *explaining* the world to each other ...'

Heathcote describes this model of both learning and teaching as a 'crucible', where teacher and students 'stir' their learning and their developing knowledge together.

It is paradoxical that, for all its commitment to open-ended learning and non-judgemental approaches to learning, much early TiE work tended to the Transmission mode, though with elements of the Enquiry mode too. The premise underlying this work was often on the lines of: 'Racism (or sexism, or the issue being addressed) is a bad thing – our work together, through the TiE medium, will both instruct and stimulate *in order to change attitudes and behaviour*.' In this respect it was closer to the aims and methods of the Alternative Theatre groups like 7:84, Monstrous Regiment, Red Ladder or Gay Sweatshop (there was a free traffic of personnel between groups like those and the TiE teams), whose work at that time was mainly polemical and supportive of political movements. In responding to that period of political turmoil and creative excitement, it frequently generated work of great power and energy. This desire directly to change behaviour sometimes even extended to the whole context of the team's visit to a school. In certain companies, it became policy to challenge, instantly and forcefully, any comments or reactions of an explicitly racist or sexist nature that arose in the course of work with school students. This was to happen no matter what disruption to the overall programme was incurred! Issues were understood as having both a political imperative that needed immediate addressing, but also a moral imperative that decent, 'progressive', civilized ideas, and behaviour to follow, should be transmitted to the audience class.

The Drama mode, however – Heathcote's 'crucible' – is necessarily more open-ended, even amoral. Its mode is scientific and exploratory and – in theory at least – would allow for the expression of 'unacceptable' or 'politically incorrect' ideas from the participants. This would be material, however uncomfortable, that would be accounted as rich and challenging as any that the company or the teacher, or most students would prefer to hear. This has an interesting echo in Bond's work. Here he speaks provocatively but soberly about *his* job:

> Is it my job to try to change Adolf Hitler into a socialist? That's absurd. I have to make Adolf Hitler more Adolf Hitler. That's what I can do ... add to the number of people Hitler will murder. That seems a weird thing but what else can I do if Adolf Hitler is there? I can't pretend to appeal to his goodness. If I have an audience where there are fascists I cannot appeal to their good nature because their good nature is already captured by society ... Theatre cannot pretend that it is somehow going to appeal to humanity. 'Humanity' doesn't exist. All you can say is what are the processes in human society that slowly, painfully and with great difficulty create democracy.

Already, here is one indication that Bond's work is likely to forge close links with Heathcote's 'Enquiry Mode', and with Theatre-in-Educa-

tion work that proceeds from this 'stirring' together learning in the
audience.

*

*Meanwhile, his mother, exhausted, was resting on the boy's bed, when an old
woman in a white smock, with beautiful long white hair, and a battered old straw
hat came into the room. It was as if the boy had infected his mother with the power to
see things. When the boy came home carrying the baby that he had taken out of the
cave, the old woman laughed at it, and him for thinking he could rescue it. And when
the boy told her about the giant and the terrible cave, she laughed even more. Then
she told him story after story about other terrible cruelties and monstrous creatures
that she knew about, and she laughed and laughed until her sides ached. The boy
was shocked and upset, but the old woman came from a time when the terrible things
men and women did to each other were so far in the past that they seemed crazy,
unbelievable – laughable!*

*

Crossroads – Roads From the Inland Sea
(A story about a school)

In 1992, a Bradford English teacher was invited by his Head of Department to suggest a playtext for A level students to study. Bond's *The War
Plays* trilogy is a syllabus option, and the teacher chose to work with
these plays. His Head of Department read the work, but after lengthy
debate and disagreement objected to the choice, describing the play
Great Peace as 'obscene' and 'pretentious', its ending a 'cop-out'. Subse-
quently he described the plays as a whole as 'boring' and his own desire
to 'punch' their author. He instructed his younger colleague to teach
She Stoops To Conquer.

There is, of course, an irony in the fact that a school Head of Department should object so fiercely to a text that is on an Examining Board's
list of 'approved' texts. More interesting is what the man found in the
plays that so rattled him. Something, plainly, disturbed him, and the
evidence suggests that it was the end of *Great Peace* that, far from closing
the play for him, actually started a great and unresolved disturbance.
This incident of course tells us a lot about the current atmosphere of
ideological paranoia in education but also suggests that in Bond plays
there is something special about their endings. To put it simply, there
are no endings to Bond plays, only beginnings.

At the Inland Sea ends with a story. It's told by the Boy and bears the
marks of the extraordinary experience he has gone through, and it is
the one story in the play that makes a real kind of sense. It contains no
magic. It can't itself save the lives of children or keep Fascism at bay.
But it is the story that opens up the end of the play. It opens the door to
something new, in sharp contrast to the doors of the gas chamber at the
end of the previous scene that open only into death. Its letting-in of
light implies new knowledge, and new action. The Boy doesn't get the

chance to finish the story because his Mother interrupts him. She's still trapped in her role as provider and martyr, but maybe there's a different quality now. The stage direction tells us she's deep in thought. Perhaps she interrupts his story because she has her own thoughts. The play ends with that enormous gesture of everyday civility, the offer of a cup of tea – enormous because the Boy now offers it to his Mother. The roles are reversed. He has the story (meaning – or the beginning of it) and can tell it, and as a young adult he can perhaps do things for his Mother.

The endings of plays say enormous amounts about their authors' intentions. In Bond's case they are often centred upon small actions that shine with significance (though this is characteristic of his method throughout any of his plays). These endings are the logical consequence of all that has gone before, though they don't wrap up the action or solve the problems offered to the audience through the play. They teem with dynamic energies and are full of potential, contradiction, the urgent necessity for new movement and activity, even when there is the appearance of disaster and stasis. Not endings at all, but beginnings. Examples are the end of *Saved* (1965), with the quiet despair of Harry's Pools filling-in (a National Lottery image before its time) set against the mending of the chair by Len. We think of Ellen and Mike in *Olly's Prison* (1992) lying together naked like newborns in their large, single bed, managing at last to understand the connections between things. We think of the dual image in *Narrow Road to the Deep North* (1968) of Kiro dying by his own hand as a man climbs dripping wet from the river, as if wet from birth, complaining that he nearly drowned. These are selected from across the range of Bond's work but, like *At the Inland Sea*, they speak of newness and potential, only temporarily thwarted.

The situation for the whole field of work dealt with in these notes has something of the dynamic contradiction at the end of an Edward Bond play. The surface situation is, on the surface, as bleak as David Pammenter characterized it in 1980. Main-house theatres have shed their permanent TiE teams, retaining, if they are lucky, some kind of Education Department and hiring in actor–teachers from what is inevitably a diminishing pool of specialist experience. What Theatre-in-Education training was offered in Drama Schools is to all intents and purposes at an end. Drama-in-Education training similarly is under pressure as the education system is restructured to reflect short-term utilitarian ideologies. Some of this destruction has been the result of economic crisis, and it is probable that this crisis is real, not some temporary hiccup in the well-ordered running of the economy. The terrible vengeance wreaked by the Right's counter-revolution of the Eighties might seem to have been rooted in pathological hatred of all that was social and communal (that hatred given waspish human form by Bond as Hatch in his play *The Sea*) but the underlying structural problems are unavoidable. The barbarians – if such they are – may have a point. The economics of the market are hard, perhaps impossible, to run without impoverishment, coercion, violence and corruption, and we must hardly be surprised if the well-intentioned and the madmen (and madwomen) alike fail to solve these problems. Cutting the Arts and Education budgets may be profoundly stupid, given the various proven cases for their 'efficiency' and 'value-for-money', but, even if it were possible to expect moderate common sense from politicians, they would in the end still find it hard to overcome the big problems posed by global markets high on technology. Market economies are, by their very nature, random, arbitrary, unpredictable and abstract – the very opposite of the human imagination, continually seeking to know, to understand, to feel, to find meaning and structure. If market economies release their energy through fission and fragmentation, socialism works by fusion and coalescence. Technology, which simply gives the market more and more tools to be dangerously arbitrary and random with, could facilitate the growth of global consciousness and activity, but instead is enslaved by global trade. (These are arguments expanded on by Bond in his *Notes on Post-Modernism*.)

Young people are bound to challenge this New World Order, consciously or not, simply because they naturally have to make sense of their world, whether it be a cot, a room or a continent. When there is apparently no sense to the answers they get, or when their evolutionary expectations are thwarted, then confusion and despair find their outlet in the dull miasma of anger, violent behaviour, pathological drug abuse, or worse still the quiet surrender of despair. All these are phenomena of the modern world that are recognized as real and problematic, but are habitually addressed as symptoms without a cause – in fact as 'sin' – and so are actually tolerated as long as they can be contained either by ideological manipulation masquerading as moral teaching, or if necessary, by outright force.

The skills of Theatre and Drama-in-Education would probably, in any sane world, be an integral part of all children's and young people's learning experience (and adults' too, come to that), and in documents such as the 'Notes on a Curriculum for Living' and the 'Programme For A Full Provision of the Arts For Society and Schools' (both published by SCYPT Journal) the movement itself has produced some far-sighted educational thinking that could locate its work at the heart of both the educational system and the educational process. That this work has been squeezed near to death in this country may be an unavoidable consequence of economic crisis, the result of outright ideological hostility or despairing liberal apathy. Or some murky compound of all of these. However, in collaborations like that with Edward Bond there is the hope – the qualified, hard, unsentimental, hope of those potent end-of-play images – that the informed heart *can* be placed at the centre of the curriculum. As these notes were written, the situation for Big Brum veered from the issuing of redundancy notices and the prospect of complete collapse to one of much greater optimism as support for the company's work from local arts organizations rallied, at least in the short term. The collaboration with the playwright is therefore likely to be renewed, and there is understandably great excitement and anticipation about this. Nationally, however, there is not a simple optimistic ending to this story. Three months from the end of the programme's run in 1995, down the road from Big Brum in Coventry, the first ever TiE team fought unsuccessfully against closure. Bond made a speech in defence of the team, part of which was published in the *Guardian* newspaper. (The whole text of the speech is included after these notes.) To adapt the actions of *Saved*, Len may mend the broken chair, but children continue to be killed, spiritually and physically. The chorus that ends Bond's opera libretto *We Come to the River*, meanwhile, has to speak for many who once worked in TiE, and the few who still do:

> We stand by the river
> If there is a bridge we will walk over
> If there is no bridge we will wade
> If the water is deep we will swim
> If it is too fast we will build boats
> We will stand on the other side
> We have learned to march so well that we cannot drown.

*

Now the boy realized that he could not save the woman or the baby from the giant and his soldiers because they had already been killed before he had ever been born. He took the baby back to the cave so that it could die with its mother. Back in his own house, the boy told his mother a story. He had learned so much that he could only tell it all in a story. And although he didn't get a chance to, he knew now that he could finish it.

*

Statement written by Edward Bond and given a first reading at the public meeting organized by Belgrade Theatre-in-Education Department on 24 February 1996

(The italicized material below was cut when the speech was published by the *Guardian*. After his murder, the media made head teacher Philip Lawrence a symbol of, and martyr to, the violence of modern society, and the conviction of a sixteen-year-old loosed a tide of manipulated concern, verging on panic, about morality and values amongst the young. The *Guardian*'s censorship seems to reflect the sheer rawness of nerves around precisely the issues that Bond and the TiE movement have been confronting all their creative lives.)

Most people asked to associate a moral institution with Coventry would name the cathedral. It is a costly 'work of art', the venue for civic and international rites condemning war and celebrating peace. Governments who make and sell mega-weapons send representatives to its ceremonies. As long as war and weapon-making are profitable – are made essential to our economy – we will make and sell weapons and go to war. Coventry Cathedral can do nothing to change that. Nor does it benefit the citizens of Coventry. Because of it not one person less is beaten or robbed, or killed, or imprisoned, or falls into debt or despair and commits suicide, or surrenders to reaction and racism. Or if they are, this might have been achieved as easily by a few priests and a few jalopies. The cathedral is a moral icon, not a moral reality.

But in Coventry there is one truly moral institution. It prevents crimes, saves people from prison, spares others despair and helps them to take responsibility for their and their community's life, and combats racism and reaction. It is not a prestigious 'work of art' but a practical force for social and individual good. Most people have not heard of it and would not know what its initials stood for. It is Coventry's Belgrade TiE.

Since it started thirty years ago, its influence has spread. Its work is copied and developed in Europe, Africa, Australasia, India, America. Its world influence has never been greater. When something is 'wrong' with children, we 'cure' them or punish them. It's a question which does them (and us) more harm! By 'wrong' I mean disaffected, anti-social, violent. Such children cannot be 'cured' because their behaviour is not a symptom of disease. The disaffection is deeper than any illness. And it would be difficult for any child not to fall into one or more of its categories because collectively the categories describe our society. The disaffection comes from their understanding that, in one or many ways, our society denies them the right to their full humanity.

TiE does not cure or punish. It does the only moral – and practically useful – thing that can be done with bewilderment and violence. It turns it into creativity. It does not stop at helping the disaffected to understand themselves and others, vital though that is. It gives them the reward that only creativity can give – the ability to change. That is something that cure and punishment can never do.

If TiE is closed, it will be replaced with a skeleton service. But it will be more dead than a skeleton. It will deal with our crisis from the point of view of the institution and its convenience, not – as TiE does – from the point of view of the child. In the modern situation that cannot be creative. It can only desperately enforce conformity – in effect the discipline of the prison house. All prisons are violent places, but the most violent prison is the imprisoned psyche.

The government knows how to deal with disaffected children when they grow up. Put them in prison and keep them there. Interestingly, in schools where the trouble starts we do the opposite: we chuck them out. Expulsion from school is a magical, shamanistic reversal of truanting. Truanting is bad, expulsion good! Shouldn't we cut out this hypocrisy and when we expel children just truck them straight off to prison? Why allow them time in between 'to find themselves'? If they cannot do this in school, how in God's name can they do it in the streets?

'Suffer little children to come unto me', the Bible says. So does the cathedral. No, send them away and lock them up. In America, a society we feverishly imitate, they kill prisoners or warehouse them for life in living graves. Yet it is a law of democracy that the more violent the state, the more violent the demos. Our leaders tell us there is no demos, no society, and (even more alarmingly) that we 'need to understand less'. The changes in education are part of this programme of ignorance. TiE is one of its victims.

It is not only the disaffected who are at risk. All children bear the same pressure. They are not becoming more 'wicked'. Indeed they and we are kinder than our forebears. Our problem is simple: a century and more ago, science began to release into society huge increments of technology and raw power. Do we think this could happen without every part of our life being changed – our family relations, war, religion, work, politics, the human psyche itself and of course childhood? Books and films are symptomatically obsessed with invasion from outer space. But the great earth-based invasion of technology and power is more dislocating than any space invasion could be. The outer form remains, the inner is utterly changed. The burden of the change falls hardest on the young. They are pioneers in a new world their parents cannot know: *their* older world has been ruined by war and the irresponsibilities of peace.

The question is not only how to make the disaffected social. It's how may normal, law-abiding people become responsible for the well-being of society so that they may make it less lawless, less an 'all-against-all', less punitive? Our democracy has no answer.

We are not made human by our reason or cleverness. Reason ran the train schedules to Auschwitz and its builders were clever. We are made human by our imagination. It is the source of our values, the faculty through which we create ourself by gaining self-autonomy and responsible social affiliation. It is not fantasy as most people think, it is the most logical of all our faculties. Through it we become either human – or inhuman. Because when the imagination is not creative it must be destructive. And it is just because it is so important in this way, that imagination cannot be taught. If it could we would not have to go through the turmoil that makes us human. Instead authority would issue its instructions, we would obey them and history would come to a stop. It's because of this that we have drama, and why drama is so important to democracy. The imagination cannot be taught – but it can be made creative. In the modern crisis that is the most important part of education. It is what TiE does.

The reduction of education to training, the frenetic activity of Thatcherism, the Sisyphean task of maintaining the economy – these are not creative responses to the crisis. They exploit it, react to it. We behave as if the economy and democracy were one and the same. The government boasts of it! Yet it is blindingly obvious that the more the economy proliferates and prospers, the more society is damaged, the more violent it becomes and the greater and more desperate its under-class. This is classical immiseration with a new twist, because now even the affluent live in increasing danger and the misery that brings. The fault-lines of our injustice are running round the globe. This is the crisis we should educate our children to meet.

No political party faces the crisis. Is it any wonder that parents can't? They welcome the 'new' education because they hope it will give their children a better chance of survival. We have lost faith. First in religion – except in the rowdy panics of right-wing fundament-alism in America and increasingly here. Now we lose faith in our ability to educate our children. We give up teaching them how to become human in the rat-race – and we do not even begin to teach them how to deal with the real crisis they will have to face.

The problems are too complex to be solved by rote learning and the sort of mechanical literacy that can be examined. Numeracy and literacy are necessary but we must go beyond them or all the rest is sterile. Each child is different, the vicissitudes of its self-creation are different, too fine-tuned to its own experience of the world to be grasped by anyone else. That is why the imagination cannot be taught. And why no child can be coerced or even encouraged to accept responsibility for its role in the world. It can only be met on its own ground: in its imagination where it creates itself.

Only drama can do that creatively. Indeed that is why human beings have drama. And this is the knowledge that TiE has made practical.

Drama may seem a negligible force to pit against the crisis. The market knows otherwise. Everything is now dramatized, lotteryized, sensationalized. Drama is the essence of post-modernism. Film and TV wallpaper the sky with drama! And it is almost all corrupt. The seem-ingly endless line of detectives ritualistically enforcing the law but never questioning morality. The voyeuristic enthralment to multi-killings.

The demonization of children. The glamorization of war. It perverts the imagination. And because so many actors lend themselves to it, they are contemptuously called 'luvvies'.

At the heart of every tyranny there is ritual, at the heart of democracy there is drama. But we have lost the one freedom without which all other freedoms, democratic and spiritual, are empty – not just the freedom to speak but even the freedom to think: we have lost the *freedom to be creative*. Our imaginations are controlled by the market, and what passes for drama is decided by accountants. That is why TiE is being shut down.

Philip Lawrence was a 'good' headmaster. Government, church, press praised him for getting to grips with a 'bad' school. I saw him on TV. On the school wall behind him hung the dramatic image of the sado-masochistically martyred Christ. He expelled sixty of his pupils. They were put onto the street. And then one day he stood in his school gateway and violence returned. He was killed. That meeting in the gateway might have been imagined by Dostoevsky in a novel or Sophocles in a play. Perhaps he was killed by one of his expelled pupils. But that would have been only a detail. I'm sure that Philip Lawrence was as innocent as his killer. But in one shape or another, violence always returns to unleash its wrath on the ignorance that creates it. And we are an ignorant society.

I do not blame a teacher for turning pupils onto the streets. The government offers no other provision. The new brutalism closes down more and more of our humanizing agencies. Belgrade TiE is among them. One day the violence this creates will meet us in the gateway.

These texts have proved helpful to me:

Books

Edward Bond, 'Notes on the Imagination' (in *Coffee*, Methuen, London, 1995).

– *The War Plays*, Methuen, London, 1985.

Politics in Performance (The production work of Edward Bond 1978–1990), Ian Stuart, Peter Lang Publishing, New York, 1996.

Selected Letters of Edward Bond, ed. Ian Stuart, 4 volumes, Harwood Academic Publications, 1994, 1995, 1996.

Learning Through Theatre, ed. Anthony Jackson. Routledge, London, 1993.

Journals

SCYPT Journal back issues (available from Deb Williamson, c/o Dukes Playhouse, Moor Lane, Lancaster LA1 1QE):

– *Rough Notes on Theatre* (SCYPT Journal No. 32).

– *The Ground on Which We Stand*, SCYPT Documents 1992–1995.

My thanks for their insights into the process to: Geoff Gillham, director; Edward Bond, writer; and all company members of Big Brum TiE. Thanks too, to W. Stephen Gilbert and Kate Organ for their observations on the play and programme.

Methuen Modern Plays

include work by

Jean Anouilh
John Arden
Margaretta D'Arcy
Peter Barnes
Sebastian Barry
Brendan Behan
Edward Bond
Bertolt Brecht
Howard Brenton
Simon Burke
Jim Cartwright
Caryl Churchill
Noël Coward
Sarah Daniels
Nick Dear
Shelagh Delaney
David Edgar
Dario Fo
Michael Frayn
John Godber
Paul Godfrey
David Greig
John Guare
Peter Handke
Jonathan Harvey
Iain Heggie
Declan Hughes
Terry Johnson
Sarah Kane
Charlotte Keatley
Barrie Keeffe
Robert Lepage
Stephen Lowe

Doug Lucie
Martin McDonagh
John McGrath
David Mamet
Patrick Marber
Arthur Miller
Mtwa, Ngema & Simon
Tom Murphy
Phyllis Nagy
Peter Nichols
Joseph O'Connor
Joe Orton
Louise Page
Joe Penhall
Luigi Pirandello
Stephen Poliakoff
Franca Rame
Mark Ravenhill
Philip Ridley
Reginald Rose
David Rudkin
Willy Russell
Jean-Paul Sartre
Sam Shepard
Wole Soyinka
C. P. Taylor
Theatre de Complicite
Theatre Workshop
Sue Townsend
Judy Upton
Timberlake Wertenbaker
Victoria Wood

Methuen World Classics *and*
Methuen Contemporary Dramatists

Aeschylus (two volumes)
Jean Anouilh
John Arden (two volumes)
Arden & D'Arcy
Aristophanes (two volumes)
Aristophanes & Menander
Peter Barnes (three volumes)
Sebastian Barry
Brendan Behan
Aphra Behn
Edward Bond (five volumes)
Bertolt Brecht (six volumes)
Howard Brenton (two volumes)
Büchner
Bulgakov
Calderón
Jim Cartwright
Anton Chekhov
Caryl Churchill (two volumes)
Noël Coward (five volumes)
Sarah Daniels (two volumes)
Eduardo De Filippo
David Edgar (three volumes)
Euripides (three volumes)
Dario Fo (two volumes)
Michael Frayn (two volumes)
Max Frisch
Gorky
Harley Granville Barker
   (two volumes)
Peter Handke
Henrik Ibsen (six volumes)
Terry Johnson
Bernard-Marie Koltès

Lorca (three volumes)
David Mamet (three volumes)
Marivaux
Mustapha Matura
David Mercer (two volumes)
Arthur Miller (five volumes)
Anthony Minghella (two volumes)
Molière
Tom Murphy (four volumes)
Musset
Peter Nichols (two volumes)
Clifford Odets
Joe Orton
Philip Osment
Louise Page
A. W. Pinero
Luigi Pirandello
Stephen Poliakoff (two volumes)
Terence Rattigan
Christina Reid
Willy Russell
Ntozake Shange
Sam Shepard (two volumes)
Sophocles (two volumes)
Wole Soyinka
David Storey (two volumes)
August Strindberg (three volumes)
J. M. Synge
Sue Townsend
Ramón del Valle-Inclán
Frank Wedekind
Michael Wilcox
Oscar Wilde

For a Complete Catalogue of Methuen Drama titles
write to:

Methuen Drama
Random House
20 Vauxhall Bridge Road
London SW1V 2SA